PROFITABLE
MAIL-ORDER
MADE E-Z

Garrett Adams

MADE E-Z PRODUCTS, Inc.
Deerfield Beach, Florida / www.MadeE-Z.com

NOTICE:

Profitable Mail-Order Made E-Z™
© 2000 Made E-Z Products, Inc.
Printed in the United States of America

MADE E-Z
PRODUCTS

384 South Military Trail
Deerfield Beach, FL 33442
Tel. 954-480-8933
Fax 954-480-8906
http://www.MadeE-Z.com
All rights reserved.

1 2 3 4 5 6 7 8 9 10   CPC   R 10 9 8 7 6 5 4 3 2

This publication is designed to provide accurate and authoritative information in
regard to subject matter covered. It is sold with the understanding that neither the
publisher nor author is engaged in rendering legal, accounting, or other professional
services. If legal advice or other expert assistance is required, the services of a
competent professional should be sought. From: *A Declaration of Principles jointly
adopted by a Committee of the American Bar Association and a Committee of
Publishers.*

Profitable Mail-Order Made E-Z™
Garrett Adams

Limited warranty and disclaimer

This self-help product is intended to be used by the consumer for his/her own benefit. It may not be reproduced in whole or in part, resold or used for commercial purposes without written permission from the publisher. In addition to copyright violations, the unauthorized reproduction and use of this product to benefit a second party may be considered the unauthorized practice of law.

This product is designed to provide authoritative and accurate information in regard to the subject matter covered. However, the accuracy of the information is not guaranteed, as laws and regulations may change or be subject to differing interpretations. Consequently, you may be responsible for following alternative procedures, or using material or forms different from those supplied with this product. It is strongly advised that you examine the laws of your state before acting upon any of the material contained in this product.

As with any matter, common sense should determine whether you need the assistance of an attorney. We urge you to consult with an attorney, qualified estate planner, or tax professional, or to seek any other relevant expert advice whenever substantial sums of money are involved, you doubt the suitability of the product you have purchased, or if there is anything about the product that you do not understand including its adequacy to protect you. Even if you are completely satisfied with this product, we encourage you to have your attorney review it.

Neither the author, publisher, distributor nor retailer are engaged in rendering legal, accounting or other professional services. Accordingly, the publisher, author, distributor and retailer shall have neither liability nor responsibility to any party for any loss or damage caused or alleged to be caused by the use of this product.

Copyright Notice

The purchaser of this guide is hereby authorized to reproduce in any form or by any means, electronic or mechanical, including photocopying, all forms and documents contained in this guide, provided it is for non-profit, educational or private use. Such reproduction requires no further permission from the publisher and/or payment of any permission fee.

The reproduction of any form or document in any other publication intended for sale is prohibited without the written permission of the publisher. Publication for nonprofit use should provide proper attribution to Made E-Z Products.

Table of contents

Introduction to Profitable Mail-Order Made E-Z™

Welcome to the world of mail-order!

Hundreds, even thousands, of dollars can come to you through the mail, every day, when you build up a successful mail-order business, and we're going to show you how to do it! You don't need complicated equipment, a lot of capital, or an expensive office to start with. But you do need determination, a place to work (your home will do fine for a beginning), and a good product.

Before you begin to sell anything, take a moment to think about the possibilities of mail-order. In order to hit the real jackpot, your mail-order business, whatever it is that you will eventually sell, must be well planned, timely, and draw lots of repeat business. You are going to have to look at what other mail-order operators are selling, to see what kinds of products sell well, week after week, in the kinds of publications that you too are thinking of running ads in. And, don't forget to check back issues of these same publications to check out which ads stopped running, which products flopped!

Remember that the better prepared you are before you actually place your first ad, the better able you will be to cope with buying, selling, shipping and all the other new responsibilities you will have. But, don't let all this talk of responsibility scare you away—mail-order is still one of the least complicated ways to get set on the road to financial independence, and possibly great wealth!

Starting your mail-order business at home

1

Chapter 1

Starting your mail-order business at home

What you'll find in this chapter:

- What product should you sell?
- How to price your product
- Where and how to advertise your product
- The "big secret"
- How to test your results

How much money do you want to make? Do you need a steady second income? Do you want to have your own business, be your own boss, and make your own decisions?

Are you ready to make a commitment to be successful—both financially and personally? The mail-order business is the way to succeed. Whether you seek to commit a small amount or all your time, and if you want the satisfaction of being in charge, financial security, or social respect, the mail-order business is for you.

Today there are hundreds of opportunities to get into the profitable mail-order business. You don't have to be creative, clever, or have invented something new. You only need the determination to achieve your goals.

What do you want from life? Are you tired of struggling to make ends meet? Maybe you're fed-up with commuting to work and living under a time clock. If you like independence, can make simple decisions easily and are prepared to devote energy to your project, **you will succeed**.

The mail-order business is not a get-rich-quick scheme. It won't make you a millionaire overnight. But it can build into a steady, profitable business at home—as big or as small as you want it to be.

Some of the mail-order companies that gross millions of dollars a year got started in small ways. Not only the well-known distributors such as Sears or Montgomery Ward, but dozens of smaller catalog houses and monthly mail-order clubs began slowly, testing ads, testing prices, acquiring customers that buy again and again as each year passes.

Think big and think with confidence. The only way to truly make a mail-order business work is to make it work for you. This is a low risk, low investment business that can return you high profits.

Seize the opportunity

note Decide how much you want to earn, how much energy you can devote to this business, and what you want out of it. You can operate a successful mail-order business in your spare time with a very small financial investment, but it's up to you to make it work.

It is a proven fact that dozens of small and large companies make great profits from the mail-order business. Although there are some who profit illegally—and get caught—the federal government promotes mail-order enterprises.

Think about what you receive in the mail. Almost every day you get flyers and brochures from all sorts of companies selling magazines, books, clothing, household items—even vacation packages. Some you may toss away without even looking at; some of them you may read; and some you may buy from, especially if you know the company and have bought before.

An honest mail-order business is something to feel proud of. As valid as opening a storefront, this business needs so little investment that, with perseverance, you almost can't help but win.

As in any other money-making enterprise, from working for someone else to owning and operating your own company, the mail-order business requires energy. But it doesn't take away enthusiasm or confidence. As a matter of fact, the more positive thought you put in, the more rewards you can reap.

What do you need?

You can run a small mail-order business out of your home from the kitchen table. All you really need is a mailing address, a few dollars for a classified ad, and a **product that sells.**

If you're just starting in this business, you don't need to invest in elaborate equipment or expensive manufacturing. In fact, you may find several products to sell that require minimum investment and bring in a maximum profit.

Once you get going, you need the usual stationery supplies such as a stapler, cellophane tape, mailing envelopes, address labels, and file folders. You may invest in a file cabinet and a desk. And, you need to use a typewriter or computer or have somebody do all the typing for you.

Eventually you may need a postal meter, good quality postal scales, and storage areas for the products you sell. Even when you establish a high profit business, you can still operate it from a home with limited resources.

How to find what sells

The basic secret to success in the mail-order business is to follow the leader. Especially when you're beginning, why should you spend the money and time to test products, prices, and places to advertise?

Start at your newsstand or library. Study every copy of each magazine that advertises mail-order products. Take a good look at the classifieds section. Write to dozens of these offers—especially any offer for something free. Take a look at the sales literature you get back. You may even purchase a few products to see what is sold for the money asked.

> *note* Consider the trends in the various magazines. You may notice several similar ads for the same products listed one after another. **They all sell.** That is where you should begin.

See the patterns?

If you review past issues of these magazines in the library, you'll notice the ads that repeat month after month. Advertisers who continue to place ads have **products that sell**. What are these products? Which ones would you like to promote?

What to sell

To be successful, you must offer something the others don't. It could be a unique product, your way of presenting the product, a new twist to an old product, something completely new, the best price—or any combination of these or other innovations.

Finally, you must find the right supplier. In the trade it is critical to deal only with a prime source—a manufacturer or direct importer (unless you can import yourself). Otherwise you will pay more for your products than your competition (a no-no). Small ads in the opportunity publication frequently attempt to appear as prime sources when they are not.

Some telltale indications of non-prime sources are: Use of an amateurish name, such as D&D Enterprises; addresses like Rt 2, Box 123, The fact that others offer the same products, and the same wording used in ads with different addresses.

Manufacturers of any size are listed in Thomas Register in your library and they can be checked out through the Better Business Bureau in their city (get the number from information and call for the address).

While you cannot be absolutely certain who advertises in opportunity magazines, check a trade journal for the subject, where the advertisers usually state whether they are a manufacturer, distributor or importer. Beware of those who import only one or two items and are middlemen for the rest.

Look through retail and wholesale advertisements for ideas of possible products and prices. Be careful not to pick something that is on its way out.

Unless you have a product (something you do or make), look for something that is new, better, cheaper, more desirable or advantageous to the buyer than products by your competition.

What products grab you? Which ones would you like to sell as a one-shot, and later as a product line? Maybe you already have a sound interest in specific products that are solid mail-order products, such as stamps and coins, jewelry or books.

Plans and kits are great to sell to decorating and handicraft publications. You may already make something at home for which you can easily write instructions and manufacture as an inexpensive kit for do-it-yourselfers.

Mail-order is an excellent way to distribute stock from a retail enterprise. If you have a store or manufacturing plant, you don't need to invest in stock. A simple brochure or catalog to follow up inquiries is a profitable way to build business.

Specialized information is one of the most profitable products in the mail-order business. Whether you sell prerecorded cassettes or small folios or booklets, you can keep overhead down and profits high. Mass producing specialized information can be surprisingly inexpensive—and there's a high demand.

If you want to develop a product line, carefully research what already sells by mail-order ads. Don't take the chance to be innovative. Others have tried before you. Take the tried and true path and sell a competitive product at competitive prices in the same publications as everyone else.

There are a few rules to follow when choosing what to sell.

- Consider the profit margin. Don't work with anything that won't bear a high markup per item. Calculating the advertising costs, product costs and mailing, you have to make a good profit for each order.

> **CAUTION** Don't try to distribute novelties, gadgets or low-cost items through mail-order. The catalog houses and other larger mail-order enterprises have that market covered.

- Consider the weight of the product and the mailability. Can you place it in a manila envelope and mail it? Padded mailers or small boxes are also easy to mail. Think twice about large or heavy items that are expensive to send.

- Is the product a regular in the publications? Do the other mail-order businesses carry this product? And does it sell profitably? Get some samples from competitors, then contact the manufacturers and find out about the profit margin.

- Can the product be sold in retail stores, and is it selling there? Unless the product is special, it won't maintain a high mail-order trade if it is readily available at the local stores.

- Do outside salespeople sell the product? Even if they are not sold in retail stores, steer away from items that are solicited for by telephone or personal sales calls. Also avoid any items that are distributed by persons from the manufacturing plants to smaller retail outlets.

- Is your product easy to advertise? In order to get inquiries through classifieds or display ads, you must be able to describe the product effectively with a few words. New inventions rarely sell well by mail-order.

> *note* A basic element of the mail-order business is building repeat business. If you keep within a similar line of products, you can sell to the same customers time and again.

Finally, consider the potential of the product. If you begin with monogrammed bags, do you want to continue with an entire line of luggage, bags and cases? Where can you go after you have success with your first product? If you are producing and distributing information, what is the potential for more products on the same subject matter?

Eventually, you'll have distributed many similar products through mail-order. You may find one product to be a seller year after year. And you may be content with that. Or, you may substitute your stock to improve the potential sales and actual profit. Think carefully about what type of product line you want to get into. You'll be living with it for a while, and you must have enthusiasm. Because it is through your product that your desires will be fulfilled and from which **you will make money.**

Don't cheat

You don't need a special permit or license to sell products by mail-order. In some states, you will need a special tax identification number and will be required to collect sales taxes. The mail-order business is changing. There was a time when some of the advertisements were come-ons for other products, fell short of their promises, or were just plain frauds.

The federal government and the postal authorities are especially strict with mail-order businesses today. Primarily because irate buyers have no other recourse, but also to clean up the industry, any enterprise even slightly suspect is investigated.

 If you are serious about operating a mail-order business for a long time, don't fall short of the law. The authorities can shut down an operation immediately, and fraudulence is prosecuted.

 It is against the law to operate a lottery or chain letter scheme by mail. Both the advertisements and the sales literature for imported products must say that the product was imported. And, you must ship within thirty days of receiving an order or offer a refund. You then have an additional thirty days grace period, but then you must refund the customer's money or ship the product.

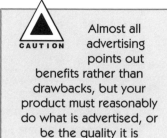 Almost all advertising points out benefits rather than drawbacks, but your product must reasonably do what is advertised, or be the quality it is supposed to be.

Aside from the fundamental laws, the authorities will judge on willful misrepresentation. Naturally, there are shades of gray in all these areas, but if your product lives up to the ads and sales literature, and you do not mislead the customers in any manner, you'll never have trouble.

Your product

 What's the least expensive way to produce your product and fulfill orders to make a high profit? If you are selling information, first test the market potential with photocopies of the report or booklet. Or, you may be able to revive an out of print publication.

If you want to distribute a product, contact several manufacturers that can make the merchandise and get competitive price quotations. Investigate ways to make the product with less expensive materials without losing quality.

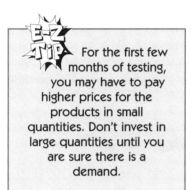 For the first few months of testing, you may have to pay higher prices for the products in small quantities. Don't invest in large quantities until you are sure there is a demand.

Check on the reputation of the firm. Is their merchandise known for quality? How soon can they deliver the goods once you have ordered?

You might try to sell a few handmade items first. Keep an adequate stock to fulfill orders, and consider mass production once the orders show the demand.

Or, you can decide to work on consignment with somebody's product that is perhaps sold elsewhere. You try the product and make the sales. You get a percentage and the other people get a percentage. Then you work out a viable business relationship.

What price?

When you investigate the products you want to sell, consider the price you can get for them. Is there an adequate profit margin? How many times might a customer purchase your line of products in a one year period?

Your profit line is the guide for deciding not only what to price your product at, but also the manufacturing costs and the feasibility of the product itself.

To test prices, you send sales literature with two prices. The results of the sales will tell you which is best. For example, if you get twice as many orders of a product at a lesser price, it will be a higher profit over a long run to keep it at the smaller price. However, if there is no big difference in the number of orders received, go for the higher price.

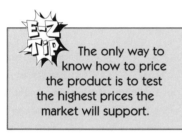

The only way to know how to price the product is to test the highest prices the market will support.

Consider the potential of your product and the product line. You'll want to expand into similar products and you'll want to make a tidy profit from the time you invest.

Where to advertise

Advertise where the competition is. If there is another classified with the same or similar product, place your ad in the same publication. Just as you followed the leaders in the choice and pricing of your product, follow the leaders in advertising.

Even though some publications cost more to place ads than others, don't try to save money in less expensive places to advertise. In the long run, your ad will pull the best responses where it's been tested and proven before.

Don't be tempted to place an ad in a magazine that does not have products similar to yours—even if you have a hunch or think it may bring in stray requests. For a beginner, follow the professionals and list where they do.

There are two types of advertising for publications. Classified ads, which are run together in a section at the back of the publication are only for words, and usually are reasonably inexpensive to place.

Display ads, or space ads, are the advertisements that run throughout the publication. They are best to use if you need to show a drawing of your product. Although they are more expensive than classifieds, your product response may do better with the extra investment.

Classified ads

Classified ads are the bread and butter winners for the mail-order business. Your dollar investment per word in a classified will pull many dollars in responses.

The best way to use classifieds is with a two-part approach.

1) First you place a small ad that describes your product or service. You give a full address and information, but mention free details, or free information. Don't ask for money or give a price.

2) From the inquiries in response to the ad, send out a direct mail piece describing your product more fully—giving a full sales pitch and a coupon. It is this sales piece that is most effective in generating orders.

Writing classified ads is easy. Do what the others do. Read other classified ads.

First there is a lead-in, or headline—a word or two that grabs the reader's attention. This is followed by a promise—some benefit the product offers. Then comes the description of the product itself. Finally, offer a guarantee and push for action. Place the classified ad in the publications you choose under the categories that seem most effective for your product. Give it at least three months to test it. Then watch those inquiries turn into orders, and the orders turn into money.

Display ads

If your product will sell better with a visual representation such as a line drawing or photograph, then you'll do best with a display ad.

You should use a space large enough to include a coupon. It has been proven that people respond faster if there is a space to fill out their name and address and place the order.

Display ads come in all sizes—from one inch to a full two-page spread. And choosing the size to run your ad will be a matter of testing the responses.

Whether it is the convenience or the simple indication of the type of information to include, mail-order businesses find that three-fourths of the orders from display ads will respond with the coupon.

As with a classified, use a catchy heading with the display ad to grab the reader's attention. Along with the illustration and coupon, describe the product and point out some of the benefits of owning it. And be sure to mention a guarantee.

The rule of thumb for deciding how big to make the display ad is to test the responses. Increase the size of the ad until it costs more than the profits it brings in. Some products don't sell any better with a larger ad; others do.

Offer a refund

An important element in all advertising, and especially in mail-order, is to offer a refund if the customer is not satisfied. The reason is simple. More people will respond to an ad that backs up its claims with a guarantee.

If a buyer can return the product for a refund, then the order is a low risk. Since your product will fulfill the promises in the ad, you will have a low refund rate. For those returns you do have, fulfill the requests promptly. Just because that specific product was returned does not mean you lost a potential customer.

Use an address code

Whenever you place an advertisement, whether classified or display, you need to code the address so you know which ad the inquiry came from.

DEFINITION

This coding system is called *keying the address*. Take a look at the classified ads you've been studying.

> *note* A simple key is the initials of the name of the publication and the number indicating the month of the issue. You can use any code that's easy to keep track of.

See those codes? Department WD-5; Division 9A; Drawer 4B. These are all address keys to use in recording and tabulating responses. They are most important in testing the pull of your ads.

You can use any combination of letters and numbers to code the address. Most businesses use the words department, suite number, room number, division or drawer.

Direct mail

Once you receive inquiries from classified ads, and start fulfilling orders from display ads, follow up with direct mail pieces that sparkle with inviting offers.

note The purpose of the two-step approach in classifieds is to get lists of potential buyers to sell to. Just as a salesperson gives a pitch with the product, you should also sell your offer with effective sales literature.

Most mail pieces consist of a sales letter, a brochure or circular, and a reply card or coupon to cut out of the circular. Many people will respond directly to the product alone and order regardless of the sales literature. For the thousands of others who want to know more about what they're buying, you have to make the difference between throwing it away and sending in the coupon and a check.

The sales letter should be personal and direct. Talk to the potential buyer honestly, telling that person the virtues and benefits of the product. Point out the features and uses. And underscore the appeal for action.

Testimonials are effective ways of selling, especially if you need to convince the potential buyer of the actual results of the product. But be sure these can be backed up by real people who can make these claims.

note Writing effective sales literature can be easy because it's standard. Look at all the other direct mail pieces you get. The same letter; the same brochure; the same reply card. These are the proven methods of selling by mail. Follow the experts and do the same.

Start small. Use colored paper to print up several hundred one piece circulars that describe your product and include a coupon. You don't have to create an elaborate four-color photograph of the product; simply describe and illustrate the benefits and features of the offer.

In a few simple words, the buyer knows what the product is, understands that it is refundable, and expects to receive what is advertised. Direct mail pieces are the best way to follow up on your customer lists. Any inquiry you receive is a potential buyer regardless of any orders made. If your first mailing didn't spark a response, follow up with subsequent mailings.

> *note* Whether you use a one-piece circular, a full-color brochure, or a forty-page catalog, include an order coupon. The coupon is the most important piece in the direct mail literature. It makes it easy to place an order.

You'll have to test to see how often these follow-ups are effective. Some mail-order enterprises mail offers several times a year; others only yearly catalogs.

The big secret

The BIG SECRET to a successful mail-order business is to sell more than one product.

The most expensive sale is the first one—because you had to FIND the customer. Now that you have him, sell him something else! Once you have accumulated a list of buyers for one product, they are good prospects for another product.

They know you, you know them, and you know what they might be interested in!

Make an iron clad rule to NEVER send out a letter or package without an offer: don't waste anything! When you ship a gidget, enclose a flier for a "whatsit," and so forth.

If you don't hear from them, send a follow-up to the "whatsit," just like you did for the original product. Since your expenses are much lower for subsequent products, you have an extra profit incentive to work on subsequent sales. Some mail-order dealers deliberately make **no profit** on the initial sale; they want the customer for subsequent sales!

Here is a sample checklist for going into the mail-order business:

1) Select a company name and register it with the city or county clerk.

2) Select a lead product and locate a reliable supplier.

3) Get a post office box and permission to use a suffix or department designation.

4) Open a business bank account and arrange to find out about incoming check clearances.

5) Prepare a sales campaign: an ad, letter, flyer, coupon and return envelope and have them printed. Do the same for follow-up correspondence.

6) Place test ads with a means to determine who answers which ad.

7) Send your letter and flyer to responders; keep careful records.

8) Send out follow-ups as needed.

9) Ship the product to customers, record the transaction on their "file" and include a flyer for another product.

10) Add the name to your buyer mailing list.

11) Repeat the ad (if it did well) or revise and try it in another paper. Repeat until you are satisfied with the results.

12) Expand to larger publications and bigger things.

One of the nicest things about the mail-order business is that there are so few rules. You can sell merchandise, your grandmother's recipes, books, courses, services or whatever—as long as you can match products with those who will buy them.

You can stay small or network with others by trading mailing lists and including each other's flyers in your mailings, or even selling each other's products on commission.

Eventually, you might consider including a toll-free telephone number in your ads (hire a service), which may pay many times its cost in extra income. If you really get big, you can hire a company to handle your marketing.

Perhaps the most dangerous mistake beginners make in this business is underestimating the cost of selling.

If you pay $500 to mail out 1,000 advertisements and get a 5% return (50), the cost per response is $10. A $100 ad that pulls 50 queries means a cost per response of $1.

Plan carefully and thoroughly—so you can enjoy a successful mail-order business.

Testing results

How do you know which ads pulled best? Which magazine gives you the best dollar-for-dollar response? What price is the most profitable to sell the product at? Which sales pitch works best? Keep a complete record of all the inquiries and orders, and make comparisons to determine the best roads to take.

Testing is the hidden feature in mail-order that determines success. And testing doesn't need to be costly or draining to your profits. The best attitude towards testing is as a game.

Draw the limits of your risks and make different turns in the road when it isn't profitable. If you consider testing for mail-order like a maze, you'll be the one to find the success. One of the best features of the mail-order business is that it doesn't require a large financial investment.

note One of the elements you need to test is the pull of the magazine ad. Compare each publication with the next. Which ones are the most profitable?

So, each step of the way that you test, going ahead with high responses and discarding low response, you have little to lose and everything to gain.

If you are using display ads, you may be testing for which size pulls the best response for the money you invested. Another element that is tested is the ad copy—especially the headings. Test a few different headlines to see which is the most effective.

The obvious thing that is tested is the product itself.

Keeping records

The way to determine test results is with a record sheet. Use a separate sheet for each address key you used.

At the top of the paper, include the vital information such as the publication the ad was placed in; what type and size of ad was used; how much the ad cost; which ad copy was used; the name of the product; the price of the product.

Separate the tabulations into two main categories: inquiries and orders. If you use a display ad, you should have fewer inquiries than directly from a classified, but you need to keep track of all responses.

Write consecutive numbers down the left-hand column. These will correspond directly to the days you received responses, starting with the first day you received an inquiry or order.

note The most clever ad at the most appealing price will do nothing if the product won't sell. If your product is not successful, drop it and try something else. It's not worthwhile to put in so much effort for something that will never make it.

The inquiries section should be divided into three columns of date received, number received and a running total to keep track of how many to date.

The orders section should be divided into day received; daily number of orders; total number of orders; daily number of sales; and totally cash sales. The totals give you an up-to-date indication of how well your ad is doing.

Create your own mail-order products

Chapter 2

Create your own mail-order products

Pick up almost any book or folio on mail-order selling and invariably you will find the same advice. When you select a mail-order product, select one which:

- Appeals to a large segment of the population

- Is not readily available in stores

- Is easy to ship by mail

- Is worthwhile

- Lends itself to repeat orders

Most mail-order writers will also tell you to try to acquire exclusive selling rights to your product. Most writers agree that a dealer has a better chance of succeeding in the mail-order business if he created the product himself.

All of this is certainly good advice. The trouble with it is that it does not go far enough. It does not tell you how to create a product that is exclusively your own. In what follows, I show you, step by step, how to create your own mail-order product.

I begin by making a very revolutionary statement. ***The first step on the road to mail-order success is not the selection of a product!*** That may sound like a very strange statement, but there are three things you must do (if you want to be successful) before you ever select a product to sell by mail!

1) Analyze yourself. You will only succeed in selling a product, or a line of mail-order products, if you really enjoy selling them, if you can be honestly enthusiastic about them, and if they are products you yourself would honestly want to buy.

2) Select your market. Once you analyze yourself, you will want to sell to people with interests similar to your own. Only then will you be comfortable in your mail-order business.

3) Analyze your market. Before you ever select a product, you should know what your market is buying, what it would like to buy, if available, and what it will buy from you, in the very near future.

Once you analyze yourself, select your market, and then thoroughly analyze your market, you will have no trouble selecting or creating a product to sell by mail. It will almost select you! Now, let's go back and study these three steps, one by one.

Analyze yourself

To help you understand yourself, sit down and, as honestly as possible, write out your answers to the following questions:

1) When I go to a newsstand, what kind of magazines appeal to me?

2) What kind of books do I really like to read?

3) When I daydream, what do I daydream about?

4) What do I do with my free time? (how do I spend my evenings? What do I do on weekends?)

5) What do I do on my vacation?

6) What one subject interests me more than any other subject in the world?

7) If I didn't have to work for a living, how would I spend my time?

8) If I could go back to college, what subjects would I take?

9) What kind of products do I like to purchase by mail?

Once you honestly answer all these questions, you will see an amazing pattern emerging. When you finish, pay a visit to your local library. Go to the reference desk and ask to see the latest edition of the *Writer's Market*. Sit down and study the table of contents, which lists all the main categories of magazines currently being printed. Decide which category interests you beyond all others. It is in that mail-order market that you will be most at home. It is there that you will be most successful.

 Now, go back to the reference desk and ask for two other publications. Either one will provide you with the information you need. They are:

• The *Standard Periodical Directory*, and

• Ulrich's *International Periodical Directory*

For the sake of illustration, say that you have a compelling interest in astrology. With a little search in the standard periodical directory, you will find the name and address of at least a dozen or so astrology magazines. In Ulrich's you will find even more, since it lists magazines published in foreign countries as well.

When you start receiving your sample copies, save them and save the advertising rate cards. They will be invaluable to you in the future.

Jot down the names and address of each and every publication. Write to each of them, on your letterhead if possible. If you don't have a letterhead, you will still hear from most of them. Tell them you are starting a mail-order business, specializing in astrological products, and ask them for a sample copy of their publications, along with their advertising rates.

While you wait for these to arrive, go to the nearest second-hand magazine store and buy a few dozen old astrology magazines. (the cost? Probably a quarter each!) Get as many different magazine titles as possible and be sure to get copies with mail-order ads in them. Issues that are ten or fifteen years old will be valuable to you, but also try to obtain some of the more current issues. You are now ready to start.

Analyzing your market

Start a notebook. Pick up one of the magazines which you purchased at the second-hand magazine store. Read the first ad. Every line of it. Read it slowly and carefully. When you finish reading it, see if you can describe what is being sold in five words or less. If you can't, go back and read it again. If you can, record your description under one of three headings in your notebook:

- Merchandise
- Information
- Service

All mail-order offerings come under one of the three headings just listed. If the ad was for an aquarian necklace, it should be listed under merchandise. If it was for a treatise on flying saucers, it should be listed under information. If it was an offer to chart your horoscope, it should be listed under service.

After you analyze the first ad, study the next ad. Continue until you have thoroughly analyzed every single ad in the magazine, including the classifieds. When you are through, you will have three lists:

1) A list of astrological merchandise for sale

2) A list of astrological manuals (information) for sale

3) A list of astrological services for sale.

As you read, watch for:

• **Undeveloped ideas**—especially in older issues, you will find really good ideas that were, for one reason or another, never developed. Perhaps the originator lost interest or didn't have the capital to develop his idea. He may have died or he may have run off with a chorus girl from Las Vegas and forgotten all about the mail-order business. If you can develop the idea, you have a mail-order product.

note You will be amazed at what you will discover when you read magazines from the viewpoint of a mail-order dealer!

• **Wholesale sources**—watch for ads that say "dealers wanted" (in more current issues, of course). Here may be the perfect source of mail-order products for you.

• **The articles**—they show you what the readers are interested in and give you clues as to what the readers want to buy. Remember the articles are doing two things—they are about subjects which the readers are already interested. They are also creating new interests in the minds of the readers. Can you create a product that readers will want as a result of reading those articles?

While researching this manuscript, I analyzed three totally different magazines from the viewpoint of a mail-order dealer. I would like to share some of my findings with you. Don't worry if the fields are different from those which interest you. Mail-order principles are the same for every market!

The first magazine I analyzed was *Astrology—Your Daily Horoscope,* December 1975. I would like to begin with the merchandise offerings.

Astrology (merchandise)

The first ad is for personalized stationary. Any mail-order dealer knows you can sell personalized stationary to any market. This dealer took a commonplace product and adapted it to the astrological market. Next to the name and address which he prints on the stationary, he prints the astrological sun sign and he calls it zodiac stationary.

The next ad is for another very common product—soap! You can buy soap in any grocery store. But, this soap is special. It has your zodiac sign imprinted in it, and it lasts as long as the soap lasts. Here is another good example of adapting a commonplace product to the special interests and desires of your prospective customers.

> *note*
> You'll be amazed at how you can turn commonplace items into red hot mail-order sellers just by taking the time to put yourself in your customer's shoes for a while.

If you are now selling a product by mail and you would like to increase your sales, make a list of the kinds of people you would like to sell it to. (for example, doctors, waitresses, farmers, gun collectors, etc.) Then, go back and ask yourself what you could do to your product to make it appeal to each individual group.

The next merchandise offering is for "Seashells for Virgos and Scorpios." Had this advertiser offered plain old seashells in an astrology magazine, his mailbox would probably be empty. Had he advertised *"seashells for astrologers,"* he might have gotten a few orders. But he made his seashells special, exclusive, and very, very desirable, because they are only for Virgos and Scorpios. He is catching the attention of one reader out of every six and I would bet that ad was a mail-order success! Here is an idea worth remembering. Try to apply it to your product!

Another merchandise offering was a *"hand bio-rhythm computer."* For the past few years, astrology magazines ran article after article on the bio-rhythm theory (i.e. Every male and female person has emotional, intellectual and physical cycles, which can be predicted in advance). The astrology magazines, in effect, created a mail-order market for this kind of new product. The ad promises, *"it reveals your emotional, intellectual and physical state— Even before the day begins!"* This dealer was clever enough to do something about this new interest. If he had not studied his market, he could never have discovered the need for a bio-rhythm computer!

Astrology (information)

Readers of astrology magazines are very interested in love, money, success, power, miracles, prayer, etc. One enterprising dealer wrote six "personal guidance" manuals, and runs full page ads in astrology magazines, selling them from $2.00 to $11.00 each! His ads have run successfully for years. Back in 1960, when I first became interested in selling by mail, this dealer was running small ads in mail dealer magazines, selling mail-order manuals!

Here are some of the other information manuals which dealers are selling by mail:

- How the Maya Indians foretold the future—$15.00

- Powerful words to be recited daily to end your money worries—$4.00

- How to spiritually heal your pets—$5.00

- A manual on etheric astral projection, written "especially for the neophyte"—$3.00

Can you create a worthwhile manual for this market? (I predict that the first dealer who writes a good manual on bio-rhythm will make a fortune!) If you need ideas for manuals, study the subjects being offered in the astrology magazines. Readers are interested in those subjects! This is only a partial list of articles I found about astrology:

- "Yearly Forecast for Sagittarius"

- "Basic Astronomy for the Astrologer"

- "Sybil Leek Analyzes Your Dreams"

- "How to Make Your Dreams Pay"

- "How Mercury Inspires Your Creativity"

A study of old astrology magazines will provide you with a wealth of subjects for new mail-order manuals (or folios).

Astrology (service)

 If there is one thing people who read astrology magazines love, it is this: They love to be analyzed and counseled by professionals. Do you have specialized training in the art of horoscope reading? If so, you can sell your services by mail. Here are some of the headlines from ads offering such services:

- "Let an Expert Discuss Your Life!"

- "This Horoscope is About You"

- "Now—A serious study of you!"

- "Now there is a horoscope written for the two of you! One for you, one for your loved one! It could mean the difference between a happy marriage and a painful divorce!"

  - "1999—2000—2001! Is one of these your year of destiny?" (this ran in an astrology magazine for at least ten years. Every year, the advertiser simply changes the dates!)

Other services being offered in this magazine include:

- personal questions answered by psychics and mystics

- spiritual readings

- tarot readings

- palm readings

- handwriting analysis

- questions answered through astro-extra sensory perception

note

Are you trained to offer such services through the mail? Or, are you interested in receiving such training? (you will find many such offers to train you in a newsstand magazine called *Fate*.) If your answer is yes, this is where you should begin your mail-order career.

The next magazine I analyzed was the November 1975 issue of *Field and Stream*. Since this magazine is aimed at two mail-order markets, hunters and fishermen, I analyzed only those ads pertaining to hunters.

Hunters (merchandise)

Men who hunt for wild game spend a lot of money on their hobby. They buy top quality hunting clothes. (who wants to go hunting in a cheap pair of jungle boots?) They spend a lot of money on their guns, their hunting knives, and on top quality binoculars. There are several dozen well-established mail-order companies selling this kind of merchandise to hunters. If you plan to establish a one-man mail-order operation, you would be well advised not to try to compete with these companies. Instead, look for something unique that a hunter can use, and begin your mail-order business there.

Here are a few merchandise offerings being made by enterprising dealers:

"Deer Hunter's Soap" (bathe in soap scented with the aroma of a female deer and you will attract a buck. Only $1.50 per bar!) Notice how a smart dealer adapted a commonplace item to a specialized market. Notice too that he adapted it to only one kind of hunter. He didn't offer it to bear hunters, to coon hunters, to quail hunters, or to game hunters in general. He offered it to deer hunters! If you are a deer hunter, you would notice that ad!

"Curtain Rods For Hunting Vans—$3.95 a pair." Sure, you can buy curtain rods in any dime store, but not curtain rods for hunting vans! Another excellent example of taking a commonplace item, adapting it to a specialized market, and creating a new mail-order product.

Also offered:

- gun cleaning cloths (10 for a dollar)
- brass nameplates for hunting dogs (not for just any old dog!)
- ID tags for your hunting dogs
- handwarmers and bodywarmers (boy, could you use these when you get lost in the snow!)

You always get more orders if you direct your ad to specific people.

There was a small classified ad offering "fish and game rubber stamps." I hope this dealer got a lot of orders, but if he didn't, I suspect it was because his offer was too general. First of all, it would have sold better with an illustrated display ad. Even better—Let us go back to the Virgo and Scorpio concept. How about rubber stamps for coon hunters? Or, for pheasant hunters? Or, rubber stamps for taxidermists?

Hunting (information)

Frankly, I was amazed at the amount of information folios being sold to hunters. Here are some examples:

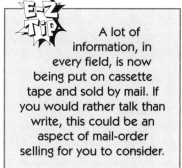

A lot of information, in every field, is now being put on cassette tape and sold by mail. If you would rather talk than write, this could be an aspect of mail-order selling for you to consider.

- "How to Build Your Own Gun Cabinet"

- "Duck Calling Instructions" (30 minutes on tape!)

- "Chart showing life-size tracks of 38 animals in the Adirondack mountains."

- "How to Build Box Traps— $1.00"

- "My 50-year-old Secret to Coon Trapping. Guaranteed, $1.00"

- "Mount Fish for Fun and Profit—Easy Instructions—$1.00"

- "Tan your own hides—hair on or off—complete, easy to follow instructions and formulas—$1.00"

- "Build (meat, fish, sausage) smoker! Inexpensive, portable—Easy plans, $1.00"

- "Wild game and fish recipes—deer, bear, rabbit, trout, salmon and dozens more—$1.00"

> **note** incidentally, not all information is written. A lot of people buy plans, diagrams, etc. To digress, recently a dealer advertised plans to build your own flying saucer detector!

Can you write an information manual for hunters? Can you tell them how to shoot ducks? Or how to hunt buffalo? Or, what to do for snake bites? Or, how to sign up for a big game safari in the wilds of Africa? If you can, write a good manual (or put it on tape) and sell it by mail!

Hunting (service)

Unlike the readers of astrology magazines, game hunters don't give a damn about being analyzed or counseled! But, if you can teach their hunting dog how to chase a bear up a tree, then they will probably pay you for your services. Can you repair their gun? Or, can you stuff and mount their catches? If so, you can build a mail-order business offering such services.

The final publication I analyzed was the *Writer's Digest*.

Writing (merchandise)

If you are interested in the craft of writing (or if you have done well in creative writing classes) you might decide to build a mail-order business catering to the needs of hundreds of thousands of persons who dream of becoming professional writers. Here are some of the merchandise offerings made to writers:

- "Copyright and Related Laws for Writers"

- "Grants and aids to individuals in the arts—1500 sources." (what writer isn't looking for a grant?)

- "I receive checks every week for features, fillers, news. Free details."

- "Gagwriters Guide"

- "Secret Way to Make Money Writing—$2.00"

- "Make Money Writing Fillers! Up-to-date Filler Directory."

- "International Directory of Little Magazines and Small Presses."

If you can produce an information manual showing writers how to write better, or how to sell their manuscripts, then write it and sell it by mail. You have created a new mail-order product!

Writers—(service)

Some of the largest mail-order businesses in the world sell correspondence courses teaching people how to write for a living. There are also a dozen or more large printing companies (called "vanity publishers" in the trade) whose sole business is printing books for authors whose works were rejected by the regular publishing houses.

To get ideas for subjects of interest to writers, study the articles in such publications as the *Writer's Digest*, the *Writer, Saturday Review,* and others.

Here are some of the services which were being offered in an issue of *Writer's Digest*:

- ◆ literary counseling

- ◆ literary criticism

- ◆ literary editing

- ◆ short story evaluation

- manuscript analysis

- article evaluation (no
  fiction)

- ghost writing

- newspaper and magazine
  reference service (authors
  often need such a service.)

- manuscript typing

> *note* If you are a serious literary person, with a gift for writing, you could very possibly establish a business offering your services to writers.

Are you qualified to offer any of these services by mail? If you are, you have found a service to sell by mail! If you are not now qualified, why not acquire professional training? Then, offer your services by mail.

In conclusion

Study your market thoroughly, and never stop studying it! Most successful mail-order people read dozens of magazines every month. They know what their customers are thinking about, what they need, and what they will buy.

Successful mail-order people are interested in the needs and wants of their customers first. They understand that if they concentrate on those, profits will flow naturally. Those who think only of profits soon pass by the wayside.

In the beginning of this manual, I asked you to write to every magazine in your chosen field. Subscribe to as many as possible. When you have created your first product, then start advertising in those magazines (which is why I said to keep their rate cards.) Never run an ad unless you can run it in three consecutive issues. Then continue running it for as long as it continues to produce new customers for you. Slowly add new (but related) items to your line. Whenever possible, expand your business by inserting your ads in new publications.

Remember these simple guidelines:

- Don't copy anyone else! You are a unique individual. Express your own individuality in your mail-order business.

There are hundreds of mail-order markets for you to explore! Analyze yourself and then select the market that is best for you.

- Create something new and exciting!

- Create something useful and worthwhile!

- Create something you yourself would want to buy!

Basic steps to mail-order success

3

Chapter 3

Basic steps to mail-order success

What you'll find in this chapter:

⏵ What you need to start

⏵ Locating the right product

⏵ Writing a successful ad

⏵ Testing your ad

⏵ Pricing your product correctly

The following is designed to provide a checklist for new entrants into the mail-order field. Each mail-order business is different, but there are common elements that apply to most mail-order businesses, as well as some specific characteristics that may vary from business to business. The following suggestions were developed to assist you in avoiding mistakes which can be costly. Apply the various points as they may relate to your specific business.

Company name

- Select a short, friendly, informal, easy-to-remember company name.

- Your personal name is acceptable, but add "Co.", "Gifts", etc.

- Home address or post office box makes no appreciable difference.

- Unless you are using your own name, it is required in most jurisdictions that a trade name is either registered with the county or the state.

- Before spending money for printing material, make sure that the name you choose is not already registered to another company. You can usually conduct a name search with an office of the appropriate jurisdiction by telephone.

- You may consider using a name that describes your product.

Company address

◆ Most mail-order businesses prefer not to use their home address as their company address. If you do, you will advertise your home address in regional and national publications. You have two other choices, a

note Most newly established mail-order businesses operate out of a home until the volume of business requires larger space.

Post Office Box (POB) or a postal box located in a commercial enterprise which rents out mail boxes.

◆ A POB is generally the least expensive, both to rent and for advertising purposes (see below). Some mail-order operators claim that it reduces business because people do not trust a POB address, yet there are just as many mail-order operators who prove them wrong. The decision is yours.

◆ If you rent a mail box in a commercial enterprise (many have sprung up in recent years), your box number usually becomes a suite number in the address.

◆ Almost all publications will charge you a full word charge for each component of your address. Example: Information Books, 300 Main Street, Suite 611, Centerville, MD 20910 or Information Books, Box 1000, Centerville, MD 20910

◆ The first address is counted as 10 words, the second one as 7 words. Since advertising costs anywhere from 50 cents to $10.00 per word (classified advertising) you could save a substantial amount of money at the end of the year.

Telephone

• Some mail-order companies do not show their telephone numbers on their stationery, others do. I believe it gives the customer some comfort to see a telephone number, although he may never use it.

note The residence phone is fine, for starters, if it is answered in a professional manner at all times.

• You can show your residence phone number in the appropriate printed material, or you can obtain a business listing for your home.

• If you plan to sell higher priced items (over $30.00), however, a business listing would be advantageous since a prospective customer may pick up the phone and check with the information operator whether "Company X" is listed.

Basic supplies

◆ Be conservative and frugal in your acquisition of items that you feel are needed. It's always wise to start small, and as inexpensively as possible. As you build profits, you can buy more and better items.

◆ A good quality typewriter or computer. (you can rent one for starters for a few months).

◆ Neatly printed letterheads and envelopes. Business stationery, business envelopes (#10's), and return envelopes, either #6 or #9 are fine. All items should have your business name and address imprinted on them. You will also need some mailing labels and some miscellaneous office supplies.

Starting capital

You should have enough starting capital to pay for the following expenses:

- Starting supplies

- Promotion expenses: Ad placement in two or three publication ads to test your offer; Preparation and layout of a display ad; Art work and typesetting of circular; Additional or continuing promotions if initial results are encouraging.

- Rental for a minimum of 1,000 names for a direct mail program, plus postage costs

- Extra capital to allow for unforeseen and unexpected expenses

Product

Select a product that, preferably:

- Is new, unusual and, if possible, exclusively yours; Is of good quality and fairly priced; Fills a definite need for a wide and ready market; Offers strong appeal to the prospect; Is not expensive to make or produce; Can be bought at low price; Interests a large percentage of the market; Lightweight; not fragile; safe and inexpensive to ship; Will be used up or consumed and must be reordered periodically.

- Is needed on an ongoing basis. Is not seasonal (except Christmas); can be sold the year around.

> **E-Z TIP** Develop a line of merchandise. It is rarely possible to make money with just one or two items. The availability of a line of related products is paramount to mail-order success.

◆ Is of acceptable quality. Know the product before you sell it. You can control its production and/or distribution.

◆ Is not widely available from retailers. The more specialized your products are, the easier you marketing becomes. If you are selling books, for example, it would be impossible, except for a very large company, to sell all types of books. You may decide to specialize in books pertaining to sports, and may want to go even further by zeroing in on football or baseball.

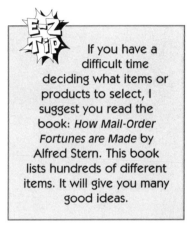

If you have a difficult time deciding what items or products to select, I suggest you read the book: *How Mail-Order Fortunes are Made* by Alfred Stern. This book lists hundreds of different items. It will give you many good ideas.

Locating a suitable mail-order item

• Look through mail-order sections of magazines to check what types of products successful mail-order dealers offer.

• Inquire of local manufacturers and Chamber of Commerce.

• Attend trade shows (with gift, jewelry, household themes, etc.)

• Contact appropriate manufacturers listed in Thomas Register, available at public libraries.

• Watch for new product listings in trade journals and magazines.

• Check out close-outs, surplus and overstock offers.

• Contact mail-order supply sources.

• Design, develop, manufacture or publish your own product.

The line

◆ Develop or acquire other items to tie in with your main product.

◆ Present follow-up offers to customers and prospects.

◆ Promote succession of products appealing to the same trade.

◆ Sell such services as personalization, consultation, etc., if such services are adaptable to your line.

Suppliers

• Develop or produce your own mail-order item, if possible.

• Try to arrange exclusive mail-order rights with the supplier.

• Establish supply sources close to home to save delivery time and shipping costs.

• Seek lowest price if item is offered by two or more suppliers.

• Order larger quantities, if you can afford such purchases, to get lower prices or greater discounts.

• Ensure the supplier is reliable and will provide the merchandise you plan to promote; that he will ship orders promptly.

• Consider only products which allow an adequate profit margin (at least a 3 to 1 profit mark-up on lower-priced items).

note It is not necessary that you make a big profit on each and every item. The real profit in mail-order comes from follow-up orders.

• Consider a supplier who is willing to "drop-ship" your orders directly to your customers—seek at least a 50% discount.

• Your suppliers should provide you with reliability, quality, and reasonable pricing.

- Since you probably should provide some type of money back guarantee (30 days is standard), you should expect the same guarantee from your suppliers.

- When buying from out of town suppliers, be sure to include the shipping charge when comparing prices to local suppliers.

Drop-shipments

◆ When you use a drop-ship agreement, available from many suppliers for a variety of products, the supplier ships your customers' orders directly under your shipping label. (suggested reading: "American Drop-Shippers Directory")

Special interest products should be advertised in special interest publications. There are a number of quality mail-order publications, but it takes time to find the right publication for your product.

◆ It is customary that the supplier guarantees not to include any of his promotional materials with the shipment; or to use your customer's name for any future mailings.

◆ Drop-shipping arrangements are suitable for people getting started. It allows you not to have to carry a costly inventory.

◆ As your business increases and you develop a sense of what sells well, you can stock limited supplies of certain fast selling items, and continue utilizing drop-shipments for slower selling products. Eventually, as your business flourishes, you can carry an inventory of everything you sell.

◆ Handling your own shipments is advantageous for the following reasons: It cuts down your shipping expenses, it decreases the shipping time, and it allows you to include promotional material directly with the shipment.

◆ When you do utilize drop-shipments, be sure to send your customer a note that his order is being processed and he can expect it by, or around a certain date.

◆ It is unnecessary to make your customer aware of the fact that the item is being drop-shipped. Include some promotional material with your letter or note.

Pricing

• Use round numbers ($3.00, $5.00, etc.) for lower-priced items to make it convenient for customers to remit payment.

• Test different prices to determine which selling price brings in the greatest amount of profit.

• Buy at a price that allows you an adequate mark-up. In setting your prices, allow for all costs: Cost of product; shipping cost and postage; bank charges including credit card charges; wrapping; bad debts; rejects; refunds, etc.; In addition, the other normal overhead costs need to be considered; marketing cost for advertising, and for printing of promotional items.

note Price merchandise fairly; give all customers their money's worth. Your prices of course, have to be fair and in line with your competition.

• The 3 biggest expense categories in mail-order are: Advertising, printing cost, and postage. Over 80% of your total expenses are in this area. Watch these expenses very carefully.

Advertising

- ◆ Don't attempt to start unless you can afford at least two or three ads; or pay for a direct mailing to at least 1,000 names.

- ◆ Plan to advertise consistently.

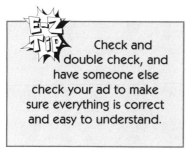

Check and double check, and have someone else check your ad to make sure everything is correct and easy to understand.

- ◆ Use ad space relative to sale price, i.e., use small-size ads for low-priced items and larger ads for more expensive items.

- ◆ Items priced over $3.00 usually do not sell as profitably through classified ads.

- ◆ In space ads, offer products in the $3.00 to $10.00 price range.

- ◆ It is usually better to advertise for inquiries if an item sells for $10.00 or more.

- ◆ Two small ads generally produce more business than one ad twice as large.

note

Sales letters should have an attention getting opening. The idea of the opening is to get the customer to read the rest of the letter.

- ◆ Repeat ads as long as they remain profitable.

- ◆ Don't waste unnecessary space; advertising is expensive.

- ◆ Don't expect to make a killing from one ad or mailing. Consistent advertising is the key to mail-order success.

Advertising expense

- • Start with classified ads. As you test them and know what is successful, you can switch to display ads.

- To test an offering and a specific ad, run it once in a specific publication. You should get a reading that could be very positive or negative. It might also be inconclusive. If that is the case, simply run it again.

note To evaluate your advertising cost, think in terms of cost per inquiry. This is calculated by dividing the number of inquiries into the cost of the ad. That cost may vary from about $0.50 to $1.30 or more.

- It is best to test an ad by running it in different publications.

- Advertise in publications that advertise similar products.

- If you have a sure seller, buy larger space.

- Keep on changing the ad and offering it until you are satisfied it is right.

- Examples of changes you can make are: size of ad, copy, appeal, special gimmicks such as discounts, free gifts or reports, etc.

- Remember: An ad can be 20 or 30 times more successful than another ad advertising the same product. It pays, therefore, to continue testing until it is just right.

- Repeat a successful ad until you no longer get a satisfactory return.

- The conventional advertising cost is 15% of sales or more in mail-order.

- Be careful when you allocate advertising funds to small mail-order publications. The ad may appear to be very inexpensive. However, a $15.00 ad that gets no response is a lot more expensive than a $110.00 ad that gets over 100 inquiries.

- Stay away from those publications that have no news or editorial content, and also those that have poor printing quality.

Advertising copy

◆ Use attention-getting, bold headline copy in ads.

◆ Illustrate the product if space permits; explain how it is used.

◆ Write tight copy.

◆ Write copy in brief, bouncy, down-to-earth style.

◆ Describe the product clearly and fully.

◆ Stress the "YOU" approach; tell how the offer will benefit the buyer.

◆ Avoid overtalking about yourself or your company.

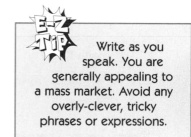

Write as you speak. You are generally appealing to a mass market. Avoid any overly-clever, tricky phrases or expressions.

◆ Strive for conviction and sincerity—be believable. Be sincere; don't exaggerate.

◆ Stir the reader to action to order your product.

◆ Give specific, clear directions for ordering.

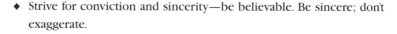

The emphasis should be on YOU THE CUSTOMER, rather than I, the company.

◆ Provide a guarantee of satisfaction or money back.

◆ Tailor the ad/literature to fit the prospect you want to reach.

◆ Prepare the ad copy with care. It must fit your specific medium.

◆ Don't make unreasonable claims, but remember that you are selling.

◆ Try to convince the reader that you are reliable and trustworthy.

◆ Key all ads to test their effectiveness.

◆ Always watch where your competitors are advertising.

◆ Experiment with new publications.

◆ It is generally considered impossible to sell something that costs more than $2.00 to

It is unwise to offer money back guarantees on items priced very inexpensively, for example, a $3.00 report.

$4.00 direct from either a classified ad or a small display ad. This is because there just is not enough space to convince someone to part with $10.00 or $20.00. It takes a full page ad to do that.

◆ Set up your own in-house advertising agency and save 15% on every ad you place.

Testing your offer

• If capital permits, test more than one magazine.

• Test more than one ad, each in a different publication.

• Try split runs if the magazine offers regional or sectional issues.

• Continue a successful ad without change until its pull drops to break-even point.

• Don't rush to change an ad that is pulling well; experiment slowly.

• Test only one change at a time: size of ad—copy—different appeal—new headline—another illustration—new price.

• Use short testimonials if space permits.

• Offer a bonus—something free or at reduced price.

• Key each ad or mailing to determine where results were derived from.

• Keep accurate records of returns from each promotion.

The advertising agency

◆ Select an advertising agency experienced in mail-order.

◆ Check their credentials; current accounts; successful promotions.

◆ Don't use agencies which represent direct competitors.

◆ Expect to pay in advance for ad placements and other services until credit terms are established.

> **note** The general consensus is that you need to mail a minimum of 1000 names to get a fair reading. 5,000 names would give you a more accurate test.

◆ Advertising agencies are not infallible. Forgive an honest mistake. Give the agency at least a second chance.

◆ Expect to pay for preparation of display ads, copy layout, and other services you authorize. Classified ad copy will be prepared without any cost to you.

◆ Extend full cooperation; go along with their recommendations.

◆ If your advertising budget is substantial, consider setting up your own advertising agency—thereby saving 15% commission, plus a 2% discount in many instances.

Ad placement

• Newspapers with mail-order sections bring quick returns and are acceptable for initial test. Results are not usually as good as from magazine ads for long-range pull.

• Use only publications with the type of readership who will react favorably to your type of product or offer.

• Unsold inquirers should be followed up with special inducements or with new offers.

- Advertise in publications which feature large mail-order sections; place ads in the same issues or sections that your competitors advertise.

Sales literature

◆ Usually consists of sales letter, descriptive circular or folder, order form, return envelope (Some offers may be effectively sold by only a sales letter).

◆ Effective sales letter must create AIDA—Attention, Interest, Desire, Action.

◆ The circular should fully illustrate or describe the product. It must provide more detailed information about the product—its uses, benefits, advantages and other special appeals.

E-Z TIP

Disregard the multi-level marketing schemes where you receive chain letters, recipe clubs, etc. They are all the same—a big waste of money—and many of them are illegal.

◆ Return envelope is an essential part of sales literature to make it convenient for the customer to mail the order.

◆ Mailing sales offers by first-class mail vs third-class mail usually shows no appreciable difference in results.

◆ Mailing envelope can feature an attractive design or teaser message to induce the recipient to open and read the offer.

Responding to inquiries

- Each inquiry you receive in response to an ad should be answered via First Class, if at all possible, within 24 hours.

- The contents of the envelope going to the prospective customer should contain: a circular, promotional flier, or mini-brochure, a sales letter, an order form (the order form can be part of the circular), a return envelope, and other appropriate information, such as a fact sheet, a free report, etc.

- In general, circulars should be limited to one 8-1/2x11 page.

- A sales letter, on the other hand, can be as long as it takes to say everything you need to say to a prospective customer in order to sell him the product.

Postage and shipping

◆ Answer inquiries to your advertising immediately and via First Class Mail. Use Bulk Mail for future mailings.

Watch your shipping weight. A fraction of an ounce can make a big difference in a large mailing.

◆ You can save a great deal of money by getting a Bulk Mail permit. The minimum number of pieces per mailing is 200. Mail must be zip code sorted. Get more specific information from your Post Office.

◆ Keep your mailing lists clean—updated.

◆ Use all the various mail classes, such as Printed Mail and Book rate.

◆ Compare costs of shippers other than the Post Office.

◆ Guarantee return postage.

◆ Use plain but sturdy packing to ship orders.

◆ Ship via parcel post or U.P.S., whichever is cheaper.

◆ Address labels with typewriter or computer; not by hand unless indelible ink is used and address printed.

◆ Specify "Return Guaranteed" on labels or package.

Printing cost

- Finding the right printing company takes time, so keep shopping until you find the right one.

- Very large printers will not be interested in your business. Very small ones, Quick Printers and Instant Printers although convenient, are generally too expensive. Their equipment is not large enough to be competitive.

- There are many medium sized printers that will give you good pricing and quality printing. Often they have the capability to help you with layout and design.

- Use whatever promotional material is available from your supplier.

> *note* Don't hesitate to use out of town printers. If you live in a high cost-of-living area, you can probably save a substantial amount of money. Many of these printers advertise in mail-order publications.

- Until you know what sells, print small quantities, even if it is more expensive.

- Use colored paper for your promotional flyers to spice up your offer. Use white paper, blue or black ink for everything else.

Payments, refunds and complaints

- Accept cash, money orders and checks.

- Some mail-order companies state in their material that they will not ship for 10 days to 2 weeks when payment is made with an out of town check. This may be an unwise practice because it can create ill feelings with your customers. NSF checks are rare. If in doubt, call your customer's bank and inquire if funds are available in the amount of $____.

♦ If you cannot obtain a credit card merchant agreement with your bank, work through a credit card clearing house. A number of these companies advertise in mail-order publications. Since these companies generally charge between 7-10%, it may be wise to set a minimum amount such as $15.00 for credit card orders.

♦ Remember, the customer is always right. An argument won is usually a customer lost.

♦ If you receive an order with an underpayment, ship the order and bill the customer for the difference.

♦ Make refunds on overpayments quickly.

♦ Most mail-order companies offer a 30 day money back guarantee. Some offer 90 days and even more.

note An increasing number of mail-order companies accept credit cards—VISA and MasterCard for payment. It is generally felt that it does increase sales, especially if you take telephone orders.

♦ Avoid C.O.D.s unless you have collected enough to cover the costs of the return, plus costs of handling and repacking the merchandise.

♦ Don't offer to sell on credit or time payments unless item is high-priced and you can afford to carry credit accounts.

Record keeping

• As in any business, it is important to keep records.

• You need records to tell you what is going on in your business; to evaluate both your revenues and your expenses.

• It is also required by law that you keep certain records.

• Keep especially good records of your advertising expenses so you can evaluate your advertising on an ongoing basis.

Mailing lists

♦ Rent names only from reliable brokers or mail-order sources.

♦ Use only lists of people who are logical prospects for your offer.

♦ Offer your names to list brokers; this is a good source for extra income.

Do no direct mailings, except to your own lists of customers and inquirers, until you have thoroughly tested a specific product through advertising.

♦ Stay away from inexpensive mailing lists, under $40-$50 per 1,000.

♦ Avoid mailing lists whose owners make unrealistic claims.

♦ The best mailing list is your own list of buyers. Second best is your own list of inquirers.

Follow-up

• The most important factor in mail-order is FOLLOW-UP. Substantial profits can be generated from this segment, if it is properly handled.

• You can generate a lot of sales by including promotional material when filling orders for customers. Other orders are generated from mailings that are made to former customers, as well as individuals who inquired about an offer in the past.

• Send out regular mailings to your customers. At a minimum, four times per year. However, you can send out mailings as often as every 6 weeks or so, if you have a new product to offer.

- Send follow-up mailings of the same or similar offers to inquirers of advertising who did not buy the first time—2-4 additional mailings.

- As you build your mailing lists and you send out regular mailings, your orders will start flowing in.

Research and education

- Be on the lookout for new products you can offer your customers.

- Study the advertising of your competitors. Request their material and study it.

- Study all mailings you receive.

> **note** Whether you are new to this field or not, to stay on top, you must continue your education by reading books and reports on mail-order and subscribing to mail-order publications.

- If you are new to mail-order, read various publications that will improve your knowledge of the field.

The customer

- Consider the customer your greatest asset. Acknowledge that he is always right; even when he isn't.

- Handle complaints promptly; write courteous explanations.

- Offer replacement if product is broken or damaged.

- Issue immediate refunds; adjust overpayments promptly.

- Promote new or other products to your customer list. No other class of prospect will be as responsive.

- Work your customer list until it no longer proves profitable.

You

♦ You, mainly, control the destiny of your mail-order business.

♦ Be energetic; devote as much time as you can spare to advance your enterprise to a more profitable future.

Refer to this handy checklist periodically—remind yourself to follow only accepted guidelines that control the safe operation of a mail-order business.

♦ Be determined to make your mail-order business a huge success.

♦ Learn as much as you can about mail-order techniques.

♦ Be original; exclusive.

♦ Don't copy just anyone; copy only the successful methods and techniques; and always strive to improve on them.

♦ Keep searching diligently for new, "exclusive" products.

♦ Don't become disappointed by a slow start, or discouraged by a failure or two along the way.

♦ Always perform professionally; an amateur does not get paid for his services.

♦ Build your own financial pyramid; reinvest profits into productive programs that may mushroom your profits steadily.

♦ Avoid being an easy mark for "get-rich-quick" schemes; start and operate your business on sound principles.

Continue to learn about mail-order by reading, experimenting, and talking with other mail-order operators. Have patience. Success will not come overnight. It takes time to build a successful business. Start slowly and expand your business from your profits.

Best of success!

The biggest key to mail-order success

4

Chapter 4

The biggest key to mail-order success

What you'll find in this chapter:

▯➤ Why you must specialize in a category

▯➤ Why you must sell a line of related products

▯➤ Why you must learn from others

▯➤ The importance of "free offers"

▯➤ Postage stamp marketing

Mail-order is a very complex business. Every phase must be planned, analyzed and tested. The right demand products must be selected; the correct type of ads must be placed in the proper media and 1,001 other details must be attended to constantly.

A great number of people enter the mail-order field every week. What they find in many instances is that only three responses are received from 100 mailings, or that a $100 ad in a magazine with 4 million readers pulls 15 inquiries, and it appears hopeless. Especially after reading the glowing ads portraying the thousands that can be made overnight from your kitchen table! The mail-order enthusiast is led to believe that he should be able to hit it big immediately with little work. When he finds that this is not the case he drops out before he has a chance to learn, fearing that it will take too much of his prime TV time, or that it costs too much to get started on the road to profits! It does cost. Much more than the $10 or $20 often advertised as the total amount necessary to put $45,000 per year in their pocket!

Many continuously make fortunes in the mail-order business. However, if they can do it and you are one who thoroughly enjoys the world of mail-order, then there is no reason why you cannot make it also.

The biggest mistake in mail-order

note Remember as you proceed on your way to ultimate success that there is no such thing as a failure—95% do not fail in the mail-order business—they just do not succeed!

Selling by mail is a goldmine, but not if you sell only one product

First, let's address the most frequent mistake that mail-order beginners make: failing to learn how the mathematics of mail-order work. It's simple. Consider all the expenses involved in selling your product: typesetting and printing your advertisement; buying (renting) the mailing list; and finally, postage. This is to name only the three main expenses.

Now, if you honestly think you're going to get rich by selling a $10 or $20 product to a few names, you are in the wrong path. You certainly could get rich selling a single product. It has happened countless times. Most probably you won't. Let's put it this way: your success would take several years. Anyway, that is not the way mail-order works.

The only way you can accelerate your growth and make money is if you sell a related line of products. Do not hesitate one moment: the people who make it big in mail-order are the ones that understand and apply this concept. The principle that lies behind this is that finding a customer is very expensive.

You sold something for $10 or $20 and then what? Do you forget about your new customer? No!! The true way to make money is to continue to supply that customer with additional related products.

There is no reason why you shouldn't do this. Sure, it's extra work. It is easier to make a sale, take the money and run. That's just too good to be true. Many folks still think that there are ways to make money the

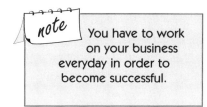

note You have to work on your business everyday in order to become successful.

easy way, with no work at all, making a million in one week and then spending the rest of their lives in the Caribbean.

Once you get a customer, it is so easy to get extra earnings from further sales that it's foolish not to offer him more products. You'd be letting go of the real bulk of your profit.

They must be related products. Here's why: If someone buys a book from you on "secret inexpensive advertising methods," it wouldn't be wise to then send him/her an advertisement on computer software. That person is now more likely to be interested in buying a report on "the biggest mistakes to avoid" or looking for renting a name list to mail out his recently published booklet. Get the picture? This is the idea of a Product Line. You don't need to offer expensive items and expensive sales brochures to follow this procedure successfully. Prepare an informative set of circulars of reports, or books, on a certain general subject like, for example, the ever popular "making money in mail-order," which is a safe subject to get into (most people are interested in making money from their homes).

The only way the small mail-order operator can find the way to big

note Mail-order is a hot business, not only for big companies but also for the little guy who starts from his kitchen table.

earnings is to specialize in a certain area. Your sales literature should offer products from a certain category, and mailed to a specifically targeted group of people. Therefore, you are minimizing expenses and increasing the probabilities of making more sales per piece mailed.

Think about this: If you mail 1000 envelopes to a list of names you just rented, it costs you exactly the same money, as if you send out a circular offering a book than if you send along 4-5 circulars offering related reports, or books, etc. OK, you spent some extra bucks on printing those other circulars, but you spent the same money on postage and on the names lists. If your potential customer is not interested in that single item you offered, you just threw away all that money. However, if you mailed out 4, 5 or 10 different offers you have a much better chance of pulling one or more orders.

In conclusion: the odds of making money are against you. They will be in your favor only when you have more than one product to offer, or better yet, 4, 5 or more. Specialize in one particular field. Target to that specific market through specialized publications or mailing lists. Conduct a decent business in order to keep people satisfied and needing to buy more products from you. If you put all this small extra effort in, you will be rewarded with a profitable share of this mail-order market.

Marketing is the key to mail-order success

Do you really know what marketing is? It's the art of finding ways to sell a product or service. But developing new ways of selling a product are not easy. You have to study what other people are doing and get ideas from them.

Get your mind in a direction to sell your product. Of course it helps if you created your own product or wholeheartedly believe in the product you are selling. Now,

E-Z TIP Listen to people who actually have something to show for their efforts. They know because they were there! Why seek marketing advice from a book that reads above your head and was only written by someone who studied the field? Go and talk to the people who actually lived it! There is a difference!

all you have to do is find the type of people that are interested in buying your product. Find out what makes people buy a product like yours. Study how others are selling a similar product.

Then, armed with all this valuable information, work out a direct plan that you'll enjoy doing. Design methods around your likes, dislikes and personality traits. It works!

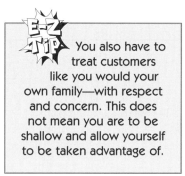

You also have to treat customers like you would your own family—with respect and concern. This does not mean you are to be shallow and allow yourself to be taken advantage of.

Even if you work outside the home 8 hours a day, you have to devote some time each evening to your home business enterprise.

Most businesses that last have seen hundreds or even thousands of new businesses open and close. That's one reason why people are skeptical of a new business until they see for themselves that they're serious. You have to prove that you are serious in order to get people to order from you and become good customers.

Customer service is nothing more than placing yourself in the other person's shoes and seeing the world and the situation from their viewpoint. Often, if you just take a few minutes to listen to people, you will learn a lot and turn a complaint into a workable situation.

In marketing, it is extremely important to start watching people and their buying habits. The next time you are standing at the checkout counter buying groceries—watch people around you. Don't stare at them, but open up your eyes and ears. Be in touch with your surroundings. Listen to ladies as they discuss the reason why they would rather buy one type of cookie over another brand name. Try and pick apart the actual reason why people react the way they do.

Here are some tips to help you appear professional and serious to potential customers in your mail-order business:

- On your word processor or computer, type a standard letter about your company. It should say something like: *"We would like to introduce our company to you. We are business professionals who are interested in providing our customers with the very best service available. We'll do our utmost to guarantee your satisfaction and repeat business. Enclosed are some offers for your consideration. They were specially selected for you and your interests. If you don't see what you're looking for—please take the time to write and let us know what we can do for you. We'd love to hear from you today."*

  Now, the next time you get a big mail or other materials that you might normally throw in the trash, you could mail your offers to these people. It only costs the price of a stamp and, who knows, they might send you $1 million worth of business over the next few years!

- Keep a list of all the mail-order publishers you come across. Then, if you ever move or introduce a new product to the market, you could send them a short press release. This works! Publishers are always looking for news to pass along to their readers.

- Give something away free for every order placed (depending on the amount of the order.) You might even want to give the customer a choice of the free items he/she can obtain for every order over $10, $25, $50 and $100. Instead of 50% off, offer to double the order. (For instance, instead of 50% off an order of 250 printed circulars—say that you'll double the order to 500 free.)

Avoiding common mail-order mistakes

5

Chapter 5

Avoiding common mail-order mistakes

Not everyone has worked in an office atmosphere all their lives. When this type of person decides to go into a mail-order business, they are not used to communicating with other dealers and potential customers. This lack of communication can close a new mail-order business faster than lightning.

Here are some tips to make your transition smoother:

1) Address your envelope properly

Use a #10 business-size envelope (not the short ones you use to write to your mother.) The envelope should contain the full name and address of the person you are writing to as well as your full name and address in the upper left-hand corner. If the letter is undeliverable because a dealer has closed due to death or illness, you will get the letter back if your return address is in the upper left-hand corner. In addition, if something should happen to the contents inside the envelope the dealer can contact you because of your return address. Try to avoid handwriting your return address.

Neon or glistening-type return labels are hard to read so try to avoid those. Plain white ones with black ink will do fine.

Sometimes these are impossible to read. If you can't afford pre-printed envelopes by all means order some address labels for $1.25 per 1,000 from Walter Drake (you know the kind that are advertised in your mail box everyday.)

2) Include a note or letter

Nothing is more frustrating than receiving an order from a customer with a check or cash enclosed with no explanation of what the person is ordering. Beginners often forget that the average mail-order dealer has hundreds or even thousands of products and services they offer. Many of those items might be priced the same. An example of a good cover letter would be:

Dear (fill in the name):

I noticed your ad in (name of publication) and would like to order your (name of product you are ordering.) Thank you for your attention to this matter. (your name and address)

You can write this information on a post-it note and attach it to your check. However, it is more professional to use a standard sheet of 8 1/2x11" paper and put your name and address at the top of the sheet. This way, if the envelope is non-readable or your return address is marked up in any way, the dealer can read your name and address and fill your order. In your cover letter you might want to mention that you are new to mail-order and appreciate any information to help you out. Often, dealers extend a helpful hand to others.

3) Don't expect your order in 2 days.

Some people see an advertisement, order an item on Monday and expect to receive it by Thursday of the same week. That is impossible. Try to rationalize that it takes 3-10 days to receive first-class mail. Then it takes another 3-10 days for most dealers to fill their orders.

> **note** Not everyone can provide 24-hour service, especially if the mail-order business owner is very busy. Some have personal lives that take up time. They don't spend every waking moment processing orders.

Most beginners don't realize that there are some mail-order people processing an average of 200-1,000 pieces of mail per day. It's hard to imagine. Most don't have employees to help. Please try and have a little patience and understanding when placing an order. If you place an order with a national mail-order house, don't they tell you to allow 4-6 weeks for your order to arrive? Give small dealers the same courtesy.

Having a mail-order business is a lot of fun. It is exciting and you get to meet a lot of great people. However, it is also a business and should be treated as such. If you are really serious and you have never had any office related exposure, at least take an afternoon to read a book you can get free at the library on starting your small business. It's well worth its weight in gold and you can start making friends and reaping the rewards of getting money in your mailbox on a daily basis.

Mail-order suppliers

Would you send Sears $20 and expect them to know what you were ordering without specifying it in your order form? Would you send your electric company a check for $15 and expect them to know what account you were making a payment on? Of course you wouldn't—so how are mail-order businesses supposed to know what you're ordering or requesting?

A note like "Send me info" is NOT sufficient enough. Remember the rule of "who," "what," "when," and "where" we learned in grade school English?

"Send me info" doesn't tell a business what you are ordering. Most mail-order businesses carry a large number of different products. If they send you information on everything they sell, not only would it cost a lot more in postage and require a 9x12 envelope, but you'll get a lot of different information on products you may not be interested in. In fact, the business may not include the information you originally requested because they had no idea what you ordered and couldn't afford to send you everything they have.

Then, to top it off, some of these people who wrote to the mail-order business requesting information will get upset and file a complaint against them because they never sent the proper information. This is a big problem we see getting bigger and bigger.

Okay. Let's be realistic. If you are guilty of inflicting pain on dealers by not letting them know what you are ordering or requesting information for, don't worry. They don't hate you and

The next time you order something, read your note or letter one time before putting it in the envelope and sealing it shut. Ask yourself if you have provided the business with enough information to process your order. That's all there is to it!

want you to slink away in shame. On the contrary. They want your business and they want to keep you happy as a steady customer.

A correct form of writing a business letter should go something like this:

"Dear (Name): We noticed your ad in (name of publication) and would like more information on (product or service). Your attention to this matter is greatly appreciated."

If you don't want to take the time to write this much, you could just cut out the ad you saw and tape it on your letterhead or a note paper. Enclose the proper stamps, money or SASE for a reply and you're ready to fold in an envelope and mail.

Mail-order dealers sometimes believe that they are alone in this business. Most dealers work by themselves, isolated from most of the working 9-to-5 world. Remember, just because most people don't see their mail-order dealers and distributors face to face, they are there. Mail-order is full of fine, upstanding and caring mail-order dealers. Every one of them is a breathing, thinking human being. They have personal problems, bad days, slow months, busy weeks and lives to lead. All have family and friends that occupy their time.

CAUTION By all means, place your RETURN ADDRESS on the outside of the envelope. I receive hundreds of orders each year without a return address and with a few dollars stuck inside an envelope. I have no clue what is being ordered and even less of a clue as to where to send it.

Everyone should support each other and make as many friends as possible. Although the world may seem self-oriented, the only person that can begin a change is the one in the mirror. Think of others and try to be more understanding. Dealers want to fill your orders and process them as quickly as possible. Let them know what you are ordering or where you saw the ad so they can send you the correct information you need the first time around.

Mail-order money-making ideas

6

Chapter 6

Mail-order money-making ideas

What you'll find in this chapter:
- The direct mail packet
- How to avoid becoming junk mail
- How to set up your own distributorship
- Big Mail
- How to analyze name lists

Quick money-makers

Run any of the following ads over your name in any publication, adsheet or circular. When the orders come in, send the customer the answer shown, or just circle the answer on one of these information sheets and mail it to them. (This gives them the rest of the ads and answers free as a bonus).

Have your local printer print a batch of these ads and answers in volume, or just have a few copies made as needed to fill each order:

Ad 1: "How to sell your old telephone book for 50 cents a page! Information $1.00."

Answer: Run the next ad (ad 2, below) over your name and fill the order yourself with the pages from your own telephone book.

Ad 2: "A page from my telephone book with names and addresses! 50 cents."

Answer: Fill the order yourself with your telephone book!

Ad 3: "One inch all-profit ads and the information they sell, Only $1.00!"

Answer: Fill the order with one of these adsheets.

Ad 4: "How to get swamped with orders for your Big Mail! Information $1.00."

Answer: Run the next ad (ad 5) over your name and address.

Ad 5: "16 All-Profit ads free in my big mail. Rush this ad and $1.00."

Answer: Slip one of these sheets in your Big Mail and mail it to them.

Ad 6: "Gross $100.00 from a $4.00 investment. Information $1.00!"

Answer: Have your local copy center print 100 of these all-profit ads and answer sheets. Sell them for $1.00 each!

Ad 7: "Start your own "Turn Key" Mail-order Business! Rush $1.00 for information!"

Answer: Write to (place your name and address here if you have "Turn Key" mail-order plans or programs to offer) for free information on their "Turn Key" mail-order programs. Send them the full information about your programs OR, if you have none available, send them one of these sheets.

Ad 8: "Name of a firm who will put you in business for only $4.00. Rush $1.00!"

Answer: If you can put them in business with one of your programs for $4.00, or convert this ad and answer sheet to a $4.00 program for them, place your name and address here. (As mentioned, you can always refer them to the name and address of a local copy center if necessary).

Ad 9: "16 ads you can run over your name and keep all the money. Full information for only $1.00!"

Ad 10: "Stuff 100 envelopes and Gross $100.00. Rush $1.00!"

Ad 11: "How would you like to receive 100 letters a day, containing $1.00 in each one?"

Answers to ads 9, 10, 11: Fill orders with one of these adsheets. (You can have your local printer make as many copies as you need or you can get them from Prime Publishers at $4.00 per hundred sets.)

Ad 12: "100 Circulars mailed with ours in our big mail. $4.00!"

> E-Z TIP
> Save! Have your printer fit these 14 ads and answers on one sheet!

Ad 13: "Letters remailed 75 cents each."

Answers to ads 12 and 13: Perform the above two services yourself.

Ad 14: "How to get free postage for life. Details $2.00!"

Answer: Advertise a good pulling mail-order plan and at the end of the Ad put "Rush $1.00 and one or two first class stamps."

Profits through direct mail

Due to the continuing increase in postage rates, many mail-order beginners, and some of the old-timers have called it quits. They believe postage costs together with soaring advertising rates have made it unlikely that a reasonable profit can be made in the direct mail business.

Delivering a sales message to your prospects through the mail is really no different than it was before the increases. Everything else has increased, perhaps not proportionately, but enough to offset the over-all increase in the total direct mail packet.

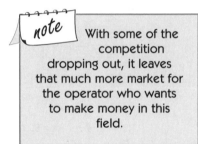
note With some of the competition dropping out, it leaves that much more market for the operator who wants to make money in this field.

The direct mail packet usually consists of a "Personal" sales letter, a circular or flyer, an order form and a return envelope. It is an offering of specific merchandise, service, or coupons to specific mailing lists. The lists include only qualified prospects for your offer so there should be a good response if you have done your homework on the mailing packet.

E-Z TIP By using third class when necessary for larger mailings and by planning the weight of your message to fit the maximum weight class, you can save a great deal over a period of time.

Direct mail provides all the space you need to influence your prospect through use of the letter and circular. In working up the direct mail packet, it is important to lay out your entire story properly at the most reasonable mailing cost.

Direct mail is an expensive method and you should test it with a series of small mailings to determine the efficiency of your mailing offer before proceeding with an all-out campaign.

In order to properly record the results of your direct mail offer, you must key your mailings so you know which ones are getting the response. This can best be done by using a different "Dept. number" on the order form, by a different color, or a different marking for each test mailed out.

Compute the results as a percentage of sales dollars or by the number of sales per number mailed. In analyzing the results of your tests, you must take into account the quantity mailed, the dates comparable offers were sent out, the kind of merchandise or services being offered, the general area of the country covered and other variances in the same or different programs.

Get results with your sales letter

A well written sales letter generally draws more response than the best brochure. The personal touch is the important difference. Direct your letter to the person and concentrate on the word "YOU"! Present the product to the prospect as if he already owns it. Let the prospects know the best points, in no uncertain terms, so they will understand fully what your product will do for them.

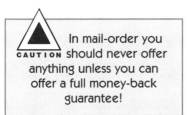

In mail-order you should never offer anything unless you can offer a full money-back guarantee!

You can't sell it unless you are confident about your product. If you are confident, you can give it a full 100% guarantee.

As with any other selling method or advertising technique, the letter must close by telling your prospect How, When and Where to order the product and must ask him to act right now!

Beware of the perpetual money-making circular program

They continue to come! The endless "money-making bonanzas"! Now there's the one called "Perpetual Circular Program," supposedly an endless money-making system where everyone wins. This "typical" plan consists of a list of 10 names, numbered from 1 to 10, indicating what each has to sell and their address.

To join the Perpetual Circular Program, you send 50 cents to each of the individuals listed, plus a large self addressed stamped envelope, which will be returned to you with their advertised offer. Then cross off the name in the number 1 position and re-number the list 1 through 10, adding your name in the number 10 position. (sound familiar?).

Next you are supposed to re-type the list and print at least 100 copies. Send a copy to each of the ten names (advertisers) and the remaining copies to names of your choice, by mail or in person.

In turn, these businesses are supposed to do the same, and as your name moves from the #10 position to the #1 spot, they state that you could receive up to 12,000,000 requests. Assuming a 5% return from all the mailers, you would receive $240,000 based on 30 cents profit per request!

> ⚠️ **CAUTION** If programs similar to this are illegal, or even if they appear to be against the law, don't touch them. These kinds of propositions never produce any money anyway. They only cost the participants' time and money, and could cost a lot more in the event the postal authorities follow through and prosecute.

By keeping the advertisers at ten, to ensure growth, they think the ads seem reasonable, at least less speculative than lotteries or fluctuating investments.

To help ensure continuation of the Perpetual Mail-order circular you can print your own mail-order ads on the back. Another way to get your ads to new sources.

Even though this plan may first appear to be merely an advertising program wherein you receive full value for your $5.00 (50 cents x 10), it is a pyramid scheme dependent on continued participation in order to produce the results it dictates. Therefore, it appears to be no more than just another of the endless illegal chain letter schemes that all of those who have been in the mail-order business for a short time receive every day of the year.

However, you can always check out this type of plan with your local postmaster who may tell you that it is illegal, even though he probably doesn't take the time to really check it out properly.

How to keep offers out of file 13

note When preparing your marketing plan and mail-order packet, spend sufficient time to work up several different attractive, but brief, messages to place on the outside of the envelope.

The best way to keep your mailing offer out of the trash can is to mail it to the right prospect.

A large percent of all mail is thrown away unopened. Most all of us in the mail-order business appreciate "Junk Mail" as it adds to our knowledge and learning process. This is not the case for the rest of the populace. The first thing they look at is the return name and address unless there is something else on the outside of the envelope that attracts their attention. When they see it's nothing to do with their business or their personal interests, it will either get a casual glance inside before disposal or go direct to "file 13" without even being opened.

If your offer is such that you can place some effective "teaser" copy on the outside of the envelope, it will be the first thing they notice and will be an incentive to see what is inside. However, if there is too much detail on the outside, they may think they saw all the message so why waste time reading the enclosures? There must be the right balance.

When they do open the envelope the first thing many of them look at is the order form to determine the price and what they get for their money. Consequently, it is of utmost importance that the wording and/or illustrations on the order form are properly laid out and attractive to the eye. Make tests and "flood the market" with the ones that pull!

How to set up your own mail order distributorship

When you develop or find mail-order products over which you have exclusive ownership or control, you may want to consider selling through agents, wholesalers or dealers. If you go this route, you should limit the number of agents and not spread your program across the country by allowing just anyone to enter. A few good agents distributing your product

When you advertise for distributors explain the exclusive features of your products and programs and how you support them 100%.

without "flooding the market" keeps them working enthusiastically and generally makes more money for them and you.

You need to develop good marketing programs for your associates, using the same general principles for the mail-order business as used in any other kind of business enterprise.

Before you start recruiting associates or salespeople, prepare a realistic packet of instructional and promotional materials, including marketing plans, camera ready circulars, photos, sample ads, sales letters and stationery, order forms and whatever else is needed to make your program a winner. Make it simple so it fits in with other offers your distributors are involved with and can be handled efficiently with little or no additional shipping or postage costs.

Make your prospect a distributor upon receipt of the first order and send out the packet with an exclusive number assigned to each one to be used on all orders and correspondence. Keep in contact with all your distributors by sending out information bulletins or newsletters announcing new products and promotional data. Build a drop-ship arrangement into your programs but try to get the distributors to carry a reasonable inventory. Give them special discounts, etc., as incentives to stock more of your products.

How to be the prime source

Information can well be one of the most profitable items in mail-order. Gathering and writing information can be one of the easiest ways to enter the field. There can be many variations by using merchandise and/or circulars of other dealers, but to actually make a big profit without including the middleman, one must compile and write their own.

A lot of thought should be given before attempting the writing project. If you are honestly sincere about writing, then set out to get the job done in an orderly and honest way.

> **CAUTION** Never try to move too fast, thinking you will get rich overnight. This is simply unrealistic. There are a certain few who try to make it by cheating the public but the law will eventually catch up with them.

You will have to spend money to pick up enough information to begin your writing project. You will have to devote much time and research in order to get started and must continue to write most every day in order to make reasonable progress.

The best kind of information to write about is that which helps others with information and advice on how to do certain things. Acquire all the information possible concerning your desired subject and study it well. You will always have the possibility to make a hit with a new idea. A good report can bring you literally thousands of dollars, even more than the big time literary and novel writers in some instances.

 The U.S. Government is a good source for certain kinds of information. They have a list of over 30,000 subjects available for a reasonable price and some are free. You can write to the Superintendent of Documents, U.S. Printing Office, Washington, DC and request to be placed on its mailing list.

Money in "Big Mail"

The amount of money you make with Big Mail depends primarily on how your programs are handled and on the materials you make available for the Big Mail Packet!

To get the Big Mails coming in, you will have to promote to the effect you are a professional mailer and for a reasonable fee will mail circulars, ad sheets, etc, to the inner circle, outer circle or both, depending on the best route for a particular offer. You can stuff many offers in a packet weighing just a few ounces.

note Unless you have a number of your own offers to include in the packet, to get started you may have to re-mail some of the big mail you receive from other dealers. They won't mind. If you are not buying perhaps your customer will. It is much better for them than to have it wind up in your file "13."

A certain amount of free mailing of commission circulars which offer good selling products can also enhance your operation by keeping your inventory of "BIG MAIL" offers sufficient to fill demand.

On the outgoing side, promote the fact you have "thousands of offers" from "hundreds of dealers" available for a small fee (assuming, of course, this is fact). This is better than using the over-worked words "BIG MAIL."

Include your own offers with all the outgoing packets. Get 100% value for the high postage costs. Fill them right to the weight limit!

Name list analysis

When considering a list offered by a supplier or dealer, ask the following questions: What is the source of the list? Why doesn't the supplier hire a "mail-order crew," use the total list and make the sales themself? Does the supplier purchase the list from another source then sell it to you at a profit?

Unless the firm has built substantial name lists, perhaps through the sale of other related products, they must buy their names from list brokers or from other firms.

If the firm buys names in volume lots, perhaps in the millions, they are entitled to substantial discounts and may even be able to offer such lists to their dealers at less than the dealer could buy direct from the same broker. In this event, certainly, they are entitled to a reasonable profit on the list resold.

> **note** It is unlikely that a substantial supplier would jeopardize the goodwill of his dealers or consumers by extensive multiple sale of name lists.

As to hiring a separate mail-order crew, in effect, that is what the supplier is doing in making his offer to dealers across the country. Except, the supplier has the advantage in that the dealers are independent contractors and, as such, the supplier has no payroll taxes and payroll expenses. Promotion and sale of their products are handled by experienced mail-order dealers, without delay and in great volume!

How to make it in the mail-order wholesale book business

note

The real profit in selling books by mail comes from having dealers sell for you. Rather than mailing thousands of your own mailing packets, at today's high postage, get thousands mailed through your own dealers. This can generate steady orders and profits and is one of the secrets to a successful mail-order book business.

There are a number of mail-order firms offering good mail-order distributorships. They offer quality books, reports and folios that appeal to the public; the kind of publications that consistently generate high profits in the mail-order business.

note You should give wholesale book selling a try. Recognize the profit potential and determine if this method fits in with your other programs.

Most of the better firms offering distributorships have a simplified program which includes instructions, profit tested literature, sales letters, brochures, order forms and return envelopes that do the selling job for you. The simple instructions can be followed even by the inexperienced person. The old timers in mail-order can use the wholesale book selling programs to supplement their other projects, in many instances combining book selling with their other mailing activities with very little added expense.

Imprinted sales literature, to solicit dealers and for the dealers to use in selling to the consumer, is furnished at reasonable prices; or camera ready copy is usually available so that the printing can be done locally. The literature for dealers is priced a little higher than cost to pay for processing the order.

The source will ship your customers' orders for literature, brochures, etc., under your shipping label. They will also drop-ship the books and publications direct to your dealers, using your name or label.

Your wholesale cost for publications will vary depending on whether you have the Prime Source drop-ship direct to your dealers, or in quantity to your place of business. The amount you charge your dealers will also vary depending on drop-ship services or quantify purchases.

> **E-Z TIP** You should make every effort to purchase publications for a minimum of four times below retail price. In other words, you purchase 100 booklets for $1 each = $100; you sell to your dealers at $2 each = $200; your dealer must realize at least double his cost when selling to the consumer, or $4 each = $400

You must ascertain that the Prime Source carries sufficient inventory with a number of different titles and that titles may be assorted in making up quantity when you purchase in volume. Determine if shipments are made promptly and if the Prime Source pays all handling and shipping charges so that your cost is "Net." Even though your cost is "Net," you must pay for shipping to your dealers; they must absorb the cost of mailing to their customers.

The price you have to pay the Prime Source often is the determining factor in the success of your program. If the book retails at a price too low, considering the high postage and mailing costs, no profit can be realized by your dealer, nor by yourself, unless orders are limited to a minimum number of titles for each total purchase. Be certain that the program offered by the Prime Source allows sufficient margin to pay for all your costs, and your dealers, while generating a fair profit for you both.

CAUTION

To find the right programs for your operation, write to a number of firms offering book selling wholesale programs. These can be found in any of the hundreds of mail-order adsheets, magazines and publications available today.

Get their literature, then order a minimum starting packet of the programs that interest you and fit in with your mail-order business schedule.

Make tests to prove the value of each program. Drop those that do not prove out after a reasonable test. When you find one that is hitting, multiply it cautiously until you know it is a winner, then go full blast in every direction to make it pay off BIG!

The best books to sell by mail

Best books to sell by mail? First, forget about fiction! These can be purchased at most any store on the corner, found at the library, or bought through the large mail-order book clubs. Scientific, technical, and textbooks are other categories to stay away from. All others have good mail-order potential. There is a broad market on religious books, especially those dealing with "End Times." However, most books in this classification are controlled by the various church outlets.

CAUTION

Self help and do-it-yourself books are best for newcomers. Adult books are profitable and repeat orders are high, but so is the penalty if state or local laws are broken. The author does not advocate selling this kind of material. One can make a fortune without resorting to what could be considered questionable material.

Mystic and metaphysical books are more or less a specialized field and generally the demand is not large. Health and recreation books have a steady market, but they are mostly tied up by firms in the catalog business.

note It's tough to sell without proper literature. Direct mail packets to follow up the inquiry are the preferable and more profitable method.

To start in the book selling business, first get sample books of the ones you think you would like to sell. Get mailing lists of book buyers and opportunity seekers; start advertising for inquiries rather than first trying to sell the books direct through the mail.

Choose the type of books that interest you the most. You can better enjoy and promote things you like. Keep card records for each of your customers. Above all guarantee satisfaction and back it up with prompt and courteous refund policies.

How to sell short reports

Several dealers give you permission to reproduce their various short reports and sales letters. You will often find some of these reports sell equally well direct to the consumer, beginners in mail-order, and to the seasoned dealers. Here are a few ways to make the most money with them:

1) Have circulars printed, listing the reports by title, selling them for $1 each, or say 5 for $3. Include a circular in all outgoing packages and letters.

2) Place small ads in mail-order trade magazines similar to the following:

   Why pay when you can get it free: Sources of Free Mailing Lists $1.00; Sources of Free Commission Circulars $1.00; How to get Cirx. Mailed Free $1.00 (Your name and address here)

3) Reproduce sales letters that sell your reports, including reproduction rights, inserting your name as the Prime Source. Mail this sales letter to your own list or one that you purchase.

4) Place small classified ads in national mail-order magazines and send the sales letters to the inquiries. A good ad for this purpose follows:

   2000% Profit, selling information by mail. Free report tells how. Send SASE (your name and address)

5) Some of these reports sell quite well from small classified and space ads. The best way to use this method is to offer a single report for $1.00 then fill the order with the report plus the sales letter which offers all of the reports and reproduction rights. Here is a typical classified ad:

HOW TO make $100 a day. Complete instructions! $1.00

In addition to giving you a small profit, these reports are designed to build up your mailing list. Generally speaking, because the reports are so cheap to produce, you can offer them free just to get fresh names in exchange. There is no need to have a large quantity of them printed up until you develop a feel for the best sellers for your operation.

The firms who initially sell you these products usually offer to print the reports and letters for a fee. For those who don't want to stock the reports, they generally drop-ship direct to your customer for 50% upon receipt of an address label and information on what reports to ship.

How to get and sell name lists

There are numerous methods of obtaining and selling name lists. If you want to prepare a national directory of mail-order operators, how do you get the listings? One way is to advertise that you are creating such a directory and will list them therein upon receiving their name and address, together with a brief description of their operations and activity.

Sell the directories by mail-order or by direct mail, nationwide, offering them at half price to those listed therein.

You can advertise that for xxx dollars you will circulate customers' names and addresses to firms eager to send them offers and programs. Sell the name lists to other dealers and firms who in turn mail offers to the list of customers. This saves money for the person wanting the offers, supplies the name list buyers with customers, and puts money in your pocket from both ends!

Here is another way to obtain name lists for nothing! An ad such as:

Big Mail? Send 200 of your address labels and $3.00. We will distribute to mail-order dealers, wholesalers, distributors, etc.!

Of course, you will be accumulating name lists from your big mail activities and from many of your other programs. The names you compile as your business progresses are very valuable. You have customers for future mailing and can also sell or rent name lists to other mail-order dealers. Retain the original envelopes received so that you have proof of names, dates, addresses, etc.

note Many list brokers across the nation have lists available for rent or sale. These lists cover every imaginable classification of potential customers for your various offers.

You should start with only a small test list to determine if it is profitable. If it tests out reasonably well, then order a larger number of the same list. If this still proves out and the orders are pouring in with enough volume to cover all your costs and show a reasonable profit, then and only then, it should be safe to multiply your earnings by going all the way with the full list that is available.

CAUTION Always remember that some lists will be completely worthless for your offer. You must test each list before committing mail-order "suicide." Be certain to choose the right category of names. If you are selling a novel you wouldn't want to mail to a list of opportunity seekers.

However, if it is a how-to-do-it type book, report, or folio, then a list of opportunity seekers may be even better than a list of known book buyers. Tests! The only way to know for sure.

All profit ads . . . you keep it all

A number of mail-order dealers publish information "folios" which they will send your customers free for a stamped addressed envelope. They provide the ads which you circulate over your own name, usually asking $1.00 or $2.00 retail. Although called "All Profit," they are really 80% commission ads or circulars. (It will cost you a first-class stamp to send the order with a stamped addressed envelope to the source, who then stuffs the envelope with the order plus ads for some of their other products.)

The source for "All-Profit" ads hopes your customer will then order something from them. Their ads cost them only the labor of stuffing the envelope and printing the materials.

You will find numerous mail-order dealers who offer the "All Profit Ads" in most every mail-order ad magazine. Send a self-addressed stamped envelope (SASE) to the various sources for samples of their all-profit ads and circulars together with full details of their offerings. Be sure to give them a test before blowing your money. Most of them are good only for acquiring name lists, other mail-order contacts, general information and for education in mail-order methods, not for direct money-making activity!

The $100 a day plan plus 6 formulas

Insert the following ad in the classified sections of local papers, in mail-order magazines, etc. It is represented (not by the author but by many of those in the mail-order business) as a quick dollar-pulling ad, but you be the judge.

Make $100 a day! How would you like to receive 100 letters a day, each containing $1.00? It's easy. Plan with directions, PLUS 6 money-making formulas for only $1.00. (Your name and address)

When you receive an order from this "dollar-puller," fill it yourself by mailing the customer a copy of this information sheet. (You can get 100 copies printed for as little as $5.00.) This is an old-time mail-order ad and is represented as one of the better pullers—but I reserve my opinion!

The Six Formulas: Make Them Yourself and Sell Them for Big Profits!

1) **Eyeglass cleaner**: Mix together 8 ounces of ammonia and 32 ounces of denatured alcohol. Put up in 2 ounce bottles to sell for somewhat less than eyeglass cleaner in your local drug store or department store. Or if you have the opportunity, sell the cleaner with your own label on it, in volume, at less than wholesale price to various retailers for resale to their customers.

2) **Mosquito Remedy:** Mix oil of citronella with common Vaseline. Apply to hands and put on shirt collar, or on a cloth handkerchief that may be tied around the neck.

3) **Liquid Hand Soap:** Dissolve any good powdered soap in boiling water. Add one part alcohol to each 30 parts of soap solution. A perfume scent may be added when the mixture cools.

4) **Powdered Hand Soap:** Put ordinary tri-sodium phosphate in sifter can, or mix seven ounces of the same with three ounces of fine powdered pumice. Retail 4 oz. bottles, or boxes for $1.00 or so.

5) **Insect and Roach Exterminator:** Mix the following: 1 pound Borax and 6 ounces powdered sugar. Add 1 oz. cocoa powder and 2 oz. sodium fluoride. Mix well. Sprinkle around places pests are known to frequent. Keep away from children!

6) **Athlete's Foot Remedy:** Mix four ounces of Borax with a gallon of water. Put up in 8 ounce bottles and sell for $1.00 to $3.00. Helps to get rid of sores on feet as well. For use on feet only.

Any or all of these formulas may be used to build an excellent home business. They are all good sellers. By mixing and packaging them yourself you can sell them to wholesalers in large quantities.

Prosperity plans

These plans are included as general information only. There are many different ones, but the basic method is about the same. There are thousands of mail-order enthusiasts taking up time with such plans. Apparently, most are legal and may be educational, or used to gather name lists, etc. But, you can spend a great deal of time and effort for very little return.

At any rate, they go something like the following:

1) Make extra money by running the following ad over your name:

   Amazing prosperity plan... Pays eight ways. Up to $6 all profit. Rush $1 for your copy today. (your name and address).

   Fill your orders with a copy of this chapter. That's all there is to it.

2) Advertise as follows:

   Receive $250 from $10 investment. Method and sample $1. (Your name and address)

   OR

   Receive $1,000 from $25 investment. Method and sample $1. (your name and address)

   Fill orders with the following information:

   250 copies of this prosperity sheet can be bought for $10 and sold for $1 each ($250). Or 1,000 copies can be bought for $25 and sold *for $1 each (That's $1,000). Order from* _____*(The promoter, dealer, or printer initiating this program would have his name and address here).*

3) Here's a $2 to $10 All-Profit Deal: Run the following 21 word ad over your name:

Choice Mailing List! 1,000 prospects wanting money making offers - 1 cent each. Minimum order 250 ($2.50). All 1,000 ($8). (Your name and address).

*(Name and address of the dealer or printer)*_____*fills orders FREE for a first class stamp plus first class stamped envelope addressed to your customer for each 250 names.* Be sure to state how many names were ordered and to be sent to your customer.

4) More all profit ads and the information they sell:

Run the following ad over your name in whatever publications you choose. When you receive orders, send your customers this prosperity sheet with the answer.

*(Name of company)*_____ *will put you in business for only $5.00. Dignified work, no ringing doorbells. Full information $1.00. (Your name and address).*

Answer them: *Send $4.00 to* _____ *(Name of the dealer or printer promoting this program), and ask for complete Mail-order Business. They will send you the program and full instructions. It's 100% guaranteed and if you wish to return the same in good condition, your full $5.00 will be refunded immediately with no questions asked! For 50 of these prosperity plan sheets send $5.00 to:* _____ *(the name and address of the promoter who will fill the order for you).*

As you can readily recognize, this could be a good deal for the dealer, printer (promoter) having others drum up business for them without any expense involved themselves.

$500 a month plan

One way to make extra money or start a business of your own is by placing advertising that pays a good profit. Selling printed information by mail can be financially rewarding. Classified advertising is the cheapest way to get into mail-order and it is often possible to raise a fortune from these small ads. Just check any large publication, such as Popular Mechanics, for their classified advertising section and you can see the many ads for yourself.

These small ads, running month after month, would not be there if they were not profitable and making money. According to some of the promotional materials being sent around the country you could make up to $500 or possibly more by running the following classified ads over your name and address. They ask you to pick up a top national publication and test either one or both under "Money-Making Opportunities" heading and watch the dollars come in. I doubt if you can make this kind of money from such a project, but for your information here are the programs and the advertisements they are talking about:

"How would you like to receive $25 daily and keep all the money? For complete set-up rush $1 to: (Your name and address)."

OR

"$500 monthly. Work at home, receive money daily. For complete set-up send $1 to: (your name and address here)"

You are supposed to fill the orders you receive with a copy of this chapter you are now reading, perhaps changed somewhat to delete the negative tone I injected! You would make photocopies or get a supply printed to send out as needed. There are other variations of this plan, but all serve the same purpose: To sell printed information to people who are interested in making some extra money. (They say it is truly possible to make money with this plan. My tests indicate otherwise).

If you study the many classified ads in the big national publications, you may get a better idea of what the leading companies in mail-order are doing. You will get a better idea of how classified advertising works.

If you have sufficient capital, some good pulling national magazines or tabloids are:

> **E-Z TIP**
> If you have limited capital, it would be wise to run your ads in smaller publications such as small newspapers, small mail-order publications, and adsheets.

- *Popular Mechanics*
- *Money Making Opportunities*
- *Salesman's Opportunities*
- *Specialty Salesman*
- *Mechanics Illustrated*
- *The Globe*

Many such magazine, tabloids and other good publications are available at your local newsstand, library or through mail-order. Many of them require a copy of the material you are selling with your ad and reserve the right not to print certain ads they feel may be injurious to the public or to the image of their publication.

Yes! You can start your own advertising and mailing business at home and keep your finances ahead of inflation, but be sure you are involved in the kind of program that gives you a reasonable chance to be a winner!

Mail-order laws, regulations, and mail fraud

7

Chapter 7

Mail-order laws, regulations, and mail fraud

This chapter provides an overview of those laws and regulations that most affect the small mail-order operator. The intent is not to give legal advice. Such advice should always be sought from an attorney. Only those laws and regulations that most directly apply to the small order operator are covered. Advice is given from the perspective of an operator of a mail-order business rather than from a legal perspective.

For those interested in an in-depth review of the laws which affect the mail-order industry, it is recommended that you read the following book: *The Direct Marketer's Legal Advisor,* by Robert J. Bosch, McGraw Hill Book Company.

The 30-day rule

To protect the consumer the FTC has enacted the Mail-Order Merchandise Rule which is generally referred to as the 30-Day Rule. Many states enacted similar laws. Some of those laws have a narrower definition than the federal; the most notable is New York State.

DEFINITION

The 30-Day Rule requires the seller to deliver the order within a 30-day period, unless otherwise stated in the sales literature. If the seller, for example, states in the order form that delivery takes 4 to 6 weeks, he has effectively insulated himself from the law. In a practical matter, however, he may have also affected his business in a negative way.

The 30-day period begins when an order arrives and has been properly paid for.

Some mail-order companies delay shipment of orders until checks rendered for payment have cleared. This should generally not take longer than 10 days. If the seller wishes to

> *note* The 30 Day Rule is an easy regulation with which to comply. It should rarely take longer than 30 days to fill an order. If it does, the seller must notify the buyer of the delay and the reason for it.

follow such a policy, he should so state in his literature. From the perspective of a mail-order operator, I do not consider this to be a sound policy. NSF and ACCOUNT CLOSED checks are relatively rare and can be minimized with proper controls. If you practice such a policy, you may save a few dollars but in return you will make customers unhappy.

I personally do not buy from companies that state in their literature that they hold checks for clearance. Most mail-order companies experience very small bad debt ratios. It is recommended that you call the bank the check is drawn on to verify funds on larger amounts; for example, on orders over $50.

Once the buyer has been notified that an order has been delayed, the seller is automatically granted an additional 30-day delay unless the customer advises the seller that the delay is not acceptable. If he does not reply to the notification, it constitutes legal acceptance of the delay. In general, and in most states, the seller may obtain a second 30-day delay as long as there is a good enough reason.

> **note** The New York law differs from the federal law in that it stipulates a maximum period of 65 days (including delays) for an order to be filled. Newcomers to the mail-order field residing in New York State should obtain a copy of the New York regulations.

The 30-Day Rule does not pertain to credit card sales. Credit card charges should be processed when an order is filled. If a mail-order credit card sale is cancelled, the seller must issue a credit against the account of the buyer within one billing cycle following receipt of the cancellation request.

Unordered merchandise

The Federal law pertaining to unordered merchandise is simple. It strictly forbids this practice. Free samples, if so identified, are exempted.

Merchandise substitution

Most states, including New York, as well as the federal law, permit sellers to substitute merchandise of similar or superior quality. The law requires it, and it is also a good business practice, to advise the buyer when making a substitution that he may return the merchandise free of charge if he is not satisfied. Certain items, such as merchandise which has artistic value, cannot be substituted. In this regard, for example, a book on how to start a given business may be substituted with a similar book on the same subject, but a book of literature by a renowned author may not be substituted.

Return of merchandise

Unless the seller specifically states that he does not offer a money back guarantee or offers, for example, a 30-day money back guarantee, he is required to make a full refund for a period of 60 days if the material is returned in good condition.

> **note**
> My own experience with returned merchandise indicates that it is quite rare. Our company, as an example, receives no more than 1 to 2 returns for every 120 to 150 orders.

If you are a seller of information products and you sell reports or other information which can be easily copied, you may wish to enact a policy stating that there is a no return policy for reports, etc.

The above laws are the only federal regulations pertaining to the sale of merchandise which are unique to the mail-order industry.

Headliners in advertising and sales literature

A few words should be said about the proper usage of some of the most common headlines used in advertising. Again, for an in-depth review of laws pertaining to advertising, refer to the book as listed above.

The most common and most effective of these terms are: SALE, NEW and most of all FREE. FREE is a magic word in American advertising used by giant companies and small ones alike. By all means, these terms should be used since they do produce sales. If the advertiser follows a simple rule of honesty in the usage of these and other advertising terms, he will stay out of trouble.

Sale

A sale is a reduction from the seller's own former selling price of a given article. The seller must have sold, not just offered the article, for a reasonable period of time. This simply means if a 50% discount is offered on a $10 book, the book at some previous time must have actually been sold at $10. If it just has a cover price of $10, but was always sold at $7, a $5 price is not a 50% discount.

Free

Free means it is free. To re-emphasize, the term is very successful and will generate sales. But, if something is offered for free, it should be free. The value of the free item cannot be hidden in another part of the offer, such as charging more for the other items than you would normally charge.

New

Here is another straight-forward term. It should only be used when new items are advertised. A new book is one which came out in the last 6 months (maybe 12 months, and that would be stretching it), but definitely not 2 years.

How to start your own company

Once you decide that you want to go into business, you must set yourself up to get started. This is not difficult. You should have no concerns on this matter. It is easy and inexpensive to do. There are no unusual legal requirements to sell by mail.

There are generally three ways to structure a business entity: The sole proprietorship, the corporation, and a partnership. The sole proprietorship is the easiest, fastest, and least expensive way to set yourself up. In most cases this would be the way to start out for a small business.

note As a rule of thumb, a business should be incorporated if it has annual sales in excess of $250,000. It is against the law in most states to use the abbreviation Inc. unless the business is incorporated. But, you may use Co.

Corporations have tax benefits that can be more advantageous than a proprietorship, but they also have strict record-keeping requirements. Partnerships also have specific legal requirements. Forming a partnership is generally necessary when going into business with someone else. There are both advantages and disadvantages in doing this. Besides sharing workloads and profits, the partners must get along well. It is almost always necessary to obtain legal counsel in order to set up a corporation or a partnership.

D.B.A. and/or business license

In most cities or towns it is required that a business license be obtained. In addition, you generally need to register your business name if you are using a fictitious name. If you are using your own name, it is not required. Call your local city or county clerk's office to obtain the necessary information.

A summary of copyright laws

For those interested in becoming self publishers either by creating their own work or using someone else's, here is a short summary of copyright law.

What copyright is

DEFINITION

Copyright is a form of protection provided by the laws of the United States (Title 17, U.S. Code) to the authors of "original works of authorship" including literary, dramatic, musical, artistic, and certain other intellectual works. Under the copyright law, copyright protection (for printed works) pertains only to the words and their sequence; it does not pertain to any idea, process, system, etc., regardless of the form in which is it described. That is, you copyright the words contained in the copy, not the content. The copyright law generally gives the owner the exclusive right to do and authorize others to do the following: in the case of printed works, to reproduce the work in various forms such as copying, etc. It also gives the owner the right to display the copyrighted work publicly.

Copyright secured automatically upon creation

The way copyright protection is secured under the present law is all too frequently misunderstood. No publication or registration or other action in the Copyright Office is required to secure a copyright. There are, however, definite advantages in doing so since, in the case of a litigation, it is substantially easier to prove copyright if registration has taken place.

note Under the present law, copyright is secured automatically when the work is created, and work is "created" when it is fixed in a copy for the first time.

Registration procedures

Registration procedures are simple. In general, to register a work, three elements have to be sent to the Copyright Office in Washington, D.C. An application (proper form can be obtained from the Copyright Office), a nominal fee, and a nonreturnable deposit of the work to be copyrighted. For more specific information, including a copy of the law, write to:

Register of Copyrights, Copyright Office, Library of Congress, Washington, DC 20559

U.S. postal laws

In general, it is against the postal regulations to utilize the U.S. mail service to transport hazardous materials, pornographic materials and chain letters involving money. For more specific information, write to:

Consumer Advocate, U.S. Postal Service, 475 L'Enfant Plaza West, N.W., Washington, DC 20260

You may also obtain a free copy of the Consumer's Resource Handbook. It is designed to help consumers resolve complaints about goods and services with local, federal and state agencies. Write to:

Consumer Information Center, Department 532, Pueblo, CO 81009

Other free publications that may be of interest to you: "Selling by Mail" can be obtained from: Small Business Administration, Washington, DC 20416-1110

"The Mail-Order Rule" can be obtained from: Federal Trade Commission, Publishing Office, #130, 6th and Pennsylvania Avenue, Washington, DC 20580-0001

A final thought: In the conduct of your business, let common sense and honesty be your guide.

What you need to know about mail fraud

DEFINITION

When the mails are used to intentionally misrepresent a product or service it constitutes mail fraud. The U.S. Postal Inspection Service is charged with investigating violations of the law, usually in response to consumer complaints.

The best way to protect yourself from mail fraud is to recognize it as fraud and not become involved. This is not easy to do because of the attractive wording in the deceptive ads.

> ⚠️ **CAUTION** Anything that sounds too good to believe is suspect. Medical formulas and gadgets that make "insane" promises are probably "insane" and you should stay away from them. Especially be cautious regarding some of the thousands of different weight loss products and overnight cures.

Never purchase land through a mailorder ad unless you or your personal representative have seen the land to determine if it is as represented and that the value is there. If the sales person showed you the property report, you can cancel your purchase agreement within seven days. If no report was shown to you before signing an agreement, you have the right to cancel within two years.

There are a number of insurance frauds floating through the mails. Requests to sign blank insurance forms, last chance bargain offers, payments in advance and cash payment requirements could indicate con artists at work.

Of course, most everyone has received chain letters sometime in their lifetime and if you are in the mail-order business you should get several every day as a minimum. Chain letters are illegal and do not work anyway. Need we say more?

 We've all seen the ads offering job placement and job opportunities. Most of them are legitimate but some are 100% nonexistent or complete misrepresentations. Don't spend your money for the required fee until you check with your local consumer affairs office or Better Business Bureau.

Then, there are those who promise huge profits without risk in commodities, stocks, oil, gold, silver or coins, through the mail or over the telephone.

> ⚠️ **CAUTION** There are hundreds of very fine investment opportunities offered, but you can't risk your hard earned cash. In some cases people have lost their life savings to mail-order or telephone swindlers.

Several of the larger, well recognized firms went bankrupt through internal fraud and management manipulations carrying their client's investments right down the drain with them. Always use caution and investigate the company thoroughly before you put up one dime.

Another favorite of the crooks is home improvements. Quite often you never see them after you sign a contract and pay them a deposit to do the work. If they send brochures through the mail and the work they perform is not as represented by the information, it could constitute mail fraud. Get estimates from local service companies to determine if the price of the mailorder offering is reasonable and in line. Check the reference of the organization.

The laws, regulations and paperwork involved in setting up franchise operations are horrendous. Various large distributorships are equally difficult to establish, but generally do not have to conform to near as many controls and regulation.

On the other hand, some mail-order distributorships and wholesale outlets require very little effort and the home company has little control over their activities.

 If profits promised are unrealistic or if the product or service is secondary to selling the franchise or distributorship, proceed with caution!

How to make $100 mailing 100 envelopes

By using the Exchange Mailing Plan, you have 5,000 3x6 commission circulars printed, the circulars offering $1.00 items and paying 50% commission on every order received. Then mail 100 each to 50 "Exchange Mailers" in 50 envelopes marked X-100SY (which means Exchange 100-Send yours). When you receive 100 circulars from each of the exchange mailers, mail out one each in 50 envelopes. This way, 100 envelopes mails your 5,000 circulars. If you have a good circular offering a popular seller, and the exchange mailers you sent yours to are honest and dependable, you should receive at least a 2% return. Then this plan will bring $50 profit.

This is the complete plan and some say it works. That it is working every day for many mailers and that it will work for you!

I have no doubt that it works; however the $50 profit mentioned is Gross Profit before any expenses. Figure it out. By the time you purchase the printing, the envelopes and the stamps, your expenses leave you little, if any, net profit.

Of course, if the exchange mailers send you top pulling circulars for their "fast selling products" and you receive 50% or more commission on orders from these, you can make a substantial Net Profit, perhaps enough to pay for your time and effort.

In this day and age of inflation and high postage costs it is difficult to make a buck by mailing circulars selling only $1.00 products. You should have a minimum selling price of $5.00 to $8.00 in order to pay you a reasonable amount!

> **note** If you are serious about making money at home, commission mailing is one way to do it, but you must have circulars that offer top selling items.

For just the postage and handling, many mail-order firms will send you commission circulars and the names of other mail-order dealers who will send you all the names you want, FREE! There are other dealers who are happy to send you their circulars without cost in order to defray their mailing expenses. All you have to do is write and request their circulars or place a small display ad in various mail-order advertisers and ad sheets indicating that you mail good commission circulars free!

> **E-Z TIP**
>
> I suggest that you order 6,000 3x6 circulars for the simple reason that most printers like to keep their printing formats and price schedules in round figures. 6,000 3x6's (approximately 2-3/4x5$^{1/2}$, not actually 3x6) will fit on 1,000 sheets of the standard size 8-1/2x11 paper.

You can get the names of a number of printers in the mail-order business who print commission circulars for a very reasonable fee.

If you handle your commission programs on a conservative basis until you have tested and proven the value of each program, you can very well make $100+ by mailing 200 envelopes with an exchange mailing plan!

What to do if you get a letter from the postal inspector

If you ever receive one of those letters from a Postal Inspector stating that the mail-order program you are promoting might be in violation of postal law or regulations, don't panic. Simply fill out the form they enclosed and send it back in. Quit promoting that mail-order program.

A letter from the P.I. simply means quit promoting the program they requested. Most mail-order programs are ordered to stop for one or two reasons. The person who originated the program promised too much and got behind on filling his orders. Or, some people became too impatient or anxious

note A lot of good mail-order programs were stopped because of one person who complained to a postal inspector. Just one dissatisfied customer can ruin your mail-order program, so keep everyone happy.

waiting to receive their order and turned in a complaint. The complaint is sent to a Postal Inspector who, in turn, sends a form letter to the person conducting the sale of the program, asking it be stopped.

Honest mistakes can happen, but remember the customer is always right. Work to fix any mistakes immediately and keep the customer informed of all progress. This, combined with honest mail-order programs, prevents those Postal Inspector letters.

The power of selling wealth

Chapter 8

The power of selling wealth

Selling products and/or services through the mail is one of the fastest growing methods of doing business. Millions of people, from all walks of life, and in all parts of the world are "into" mail-order, with more coming in every day. Some of them are grossing in the millions, others are chalking up sales figures of several hundred per month, and there are others who only give it a quick try, make a few dollars and drop out.

> *note* Mail-order selling appeals to almost everybody with a desire to get rich. Generally, it doesn't require complicated equipment, a lot of start-up capital, or an expensive office.

Mail-order is a kind of business that can be run by anyone from the comforts of their own home. About all that's required for success in mail-order selling is an understanding of what you're doing—it's not a game or a kind of thing you want to just give a quick try. It's a way of doing business, and requires a good understanding of what people buy, why they buy, and an operational plan that will lead you to success.

note

In order to make it big in mail-order, you must understand that it's a selling business. Thus, you've got to decide on what you want to sell—who your buyers will be—and know why they buy. Then, program your selling efforts in such a way that these people will buy from you.

note The bottom line is simply that everybody in the world wants to know how they can get rich—without putting forth too much of an investment in either money, time or effort.

The best, and the easiest selling product or service—because it has the greatest appeal to the most number of people—is information that "gives people knowledge or instructions" that will enable them to get rich.

So, the first thing that you should do is some marketing research: Look in all the publications running mail-order advertisements and opportunities—get a good understanding of what they are doing—how they are doing it and then formulate a business plan of your own that will allow you to duplicate what they're doing.

With get rich information or instructions—and knowing that to make the really big money you have to be the author or a prime distributor—there are two ways to go. You can become the author with all the involved headaches and demands upon your time, or you can buy the reproduction rights and re-sell or distribute them as your own.

note

As the author, you have to do the research, the writing, the printing, advertising, and order fulfillment.

As a prime distributor, you can pay a one-time fee for the reproductions rights—then spend your time and money on selling efforts. You still have to handle the printing, the advertising, and order fulfillment—but, you have the advantage of choosing and picking only what you feel will make money.

With most writers, only about 10% of what they spend hours, weeks, even months researching and writing, ever sells for them. Writers are just not geared to the profitable marketing of their materials.

Your initial marketing research should give you a good idea of what is selling—what the people are buying—and which titles of any particular author you want to promote, and sell for your own profits.

The next thing is to look through all the publications you can find that carry mail-order ads—those that run issue after issue—but not those run as fillers by the publisher—they are usually the ones that are making money for the people selling them.

Decide which kind of program you want to run, and how you want to make money. The best ad to run is one that offers a free report relative to a money making plan. You ad might read: FREE REPORT! Secret Steps to Multi-Level Marketing Riches. Send SASE to (your name and address).

In reply to each of the responses you get to this ad, you send them a one page report that briefly explains your multi-level secrets, with an invitation at the bottom for those really interested in multi-level marketing, to send in another $5 or $20 for your complete multi-level marketing "how-to" manual. You can then fill up their SASE with other offers, such as the availability of mailing lists for rent, a multi-level program of your own, and a listing of other business success reports you're offering.

At the same time, you compile the names and addresses of all the people sending for either your free report or their own materials, and you have the beginnings of a mailing list of your own that you can rent out over and over again at huge profits to yourself.

Clip the stamps off the envelopes as you receive them, and save them in an old shoe box. When you have a box full, you can sell them to any number of stamp collectors, and pocket an easy $10 to $15.

Save all the envelopes with return addresses, and when you accumulate a thousand or two of these, you can send them in to list compilers and pocket another $50 to $100.

The other way of advertising is the offering of your report or book for sales from the ad. Such an ad reads like this: SECRET STEPS TO MULTI-LEVEL RICHES! Dynamic new report shows you the easy way! Send $3 to (your name and address).

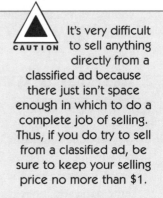

It's very difficult to sell anything directly from a classified ad because there just isn't space enough in which to do a complete job of selling. Thus, if you do try to sell from a classified ad, be sure to keep your selling price no more than $1.

A $1 item should pull well with a classified ad—a $5 item will take at least a one inch display ad—a $20 item will take a well-written full page ad, and anything more than $20 will require a professionally written sales letter.

When you're just getting started in mail-order selling, stick to small classified ads—test the pulling power of your ad, and your product, as well as the publication your ad runs in.

Analyze and practice rewriting some of the ads other people are running—experiment, and run a few ads in only one or two publications—and then build upon your success. In other words, if your first ad costs you $30, and you take in $90—take that $90 and run the same ad again, not only in the same publication, but in a couple of other publications as well. Use your profits to expand the exposure of your offer—let as many people as possible see it.

It's important to note that you cannot expect to "live off" the income from your beginning business efforts. You have to have "other" money to pay your lights, water, and gas bills.

Mail-order success is built upon the wise investment of your advertising dollars. Take $100 and run a classified ad for your reports in one of the big, national publications. Figuring that from that first $100, you take in $300, run the same ad again in that publication, and at the same time, in two other publications. Thus, your real profits should triple—and if you keep on reinvesting your profits in additional advertising exposure—conceivably within six months or less, you should be hauling in several thousand dollars per month in profits.

Insider's guide to mail-order riches

With the millions of words printed every day about "How To Achieve Success," why aren't there more new millionaires?

It's simply because the people reading this "How-To" information don't understand what they read, or don't have the drive it takes to put what they've read into action. In truth, it seems that everyone wants to "find out how to become rich," but the people with the drive it takes to work a plan, are few and far between. The basics to getting rich can be stated as follows:

• **Control your investment.** This is the key to building a fortune from small capital. You must have the ability and knowledge to make the right moves at the right time, and above all, the innate talent it takes to always land on your feet and never be wiped out, regardless of the setbacks you may encounter.

• **Know how and where to buy for next to nothing**—or produce a product from scratch—and sell at a tremendous profit. With this ability, you can start with $100 or less, and sell it to someone else for much more than you paid for it. Then do it again, and keep on doing it until you have enough money to make substantial investments in other areas where your money will grow and prosper.

- **Buy things that appreciate in value.** In other words, learn to buy things that will grow in value as time goes on. Things such as collectibles, land, precious metals and stones. Think of the multiplication factor: You pay $10 for a copyright, sell 500 copies and you're off to a small fortune.

Become an expert in your field of selling—know all there is to know about it. It takes time, effort, and energy, but the financial rewards are worth it.

- **Be choosy.** Buy the original or pick a limited field. For instance, if you buy written material, buy from the author; or if you're into stamps or coins, work with just one country or type of coins/stamps.

- **Work the tax shelters.** In the tax economy we operate in today, anyone attempting to make important money has to operate with every available tax break. There are many, and they can be applied in different ways. Make friends with a good tax accountant; the accountant can give you many angles that you probably never heard of. Take every advantage of capital gains, investment credits, take part of your rent or house payment as an office expense, as well as your car—get all you can. It's legal, and it's necessary if you're going to build your capital.

- **Set goals and dedicate yourself to attaining those goals.** In just about any buy/sell program, you can set a rate of 20% net profit on each transaction, and work a five-time-a-year turnover. This doubles your capital each year. The net profit means just that—what is yours after all expenses and taxes are paid—so you have to get about 35 to 40% markup on each cycle. If you did your homework and are really an expert in your field, you'll often make profits of 200% and more on a single transaction, because real buys show up for the person with cash in hand. If you set a goal such as this, and follow this system starting with $100, in 10 years you may have over $50,000 in cash or its equivalent.

• **Learn to exercise patience.** This is the greatest attribute of a good hunter. In your field you'll look for bargains that can quickly be resold for a substantial profit. You have to learn the sources of the items you want to sell, how to spot the bargains, and then have the persistence to allow your investment to pay off for you.

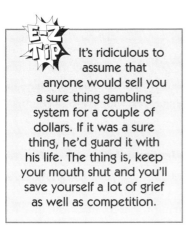

It's ridiculous to assume that anyone would sell you a sure thing gambling system for a couple of dollars. If it was a sure thing, he'd guard it with his life. The thing is, keep your mouth shut and you'll save yourself a lot of grief as well as competition.

• **Learn what to do with your riches.** When your capital has grown beyond the needs of your operation, put it to work. Get it into other investments that produce more capital and even more income. Pyramiding your investments brings you all the money you can use.

• **Keep your mouth shut!** The man with a method of making money, who understands what it can mean, keeps his mouth shut about it.

If this sounds like oversimplified hogwash, then you're missing the boat. Most people are so wrapped up in their own efforts—their own small little worlds—that they refuse to "picture and visualize" precisely how an idea or a program can or could be worked to amass a fortune. These same people, when the mood hits them, deal with, buy from, and pay an expert for the knowledge they refuse to understand or believe. The opportunity is there; all it needs is someone to grab it and run with it!

How to sell information by mail

Chapter 9

How to sell information by mail

Selling information by mail is surely one of the most profitable business operations in this country today. You can start a small business for yourself and make it flourish.

> **note** The advantages of your own business are endless, but most of all, you have a feeling of accomplishment and fulfillment, as you help other people acquire the knowledge they want—and will pay for.

You don't have to be a writer or have experience in running a business. All the steps in setting up a mail-order business are simple, easy to follow, and may reap a steady second income for you—even building up to a highly profitable full-time enterprise.

You don't need to give up anything. All the tips given in the following pages require minimum expense, can be done at home, and need only a small—but constant—amount of your time.

What you do need is the desire to make it work. If you have perseverance to follow through, and the discipline to complete each of the steps, then you are well on your way to creating something special for yourself.

Why sell information?

Bookstores mostly cater to mass market books and paperbacks; record stores carry only popular recording artists. Where can you get information on a specific topic? Even specialized magazines are limited in their scope and the information they cover.

You can order items by mail in the safety and privacy of your own home. You don't have to shop around at the stores, wasting time and gasoline. You have a direct connection with the seller of the information, often being able to write specific questions and getting feedback—especially with newsletters and courses.

Mail-order at home provides a high profit margin. Producing written or recorded information is inexpensive compared to the price you can receive. You can operate with a low overhead, the business is simple to run, and there is no middle seller. Checks come directly to you.

note People achieve success because they know something special. Specialized knowledge and "how to" are the most sought-after types of information successfully sold by mail-order.

What can I sell?

There is an endless need for specialized information that you probably have on hand, or can easily obtain. You don't have to be an expert to produce and sell that information.

Specialized information may be anything from a favorite set of recipes to a list of the fastest horse tracks in the country. It can include places to visit, such as back roads, country inns or fine restaurants in an area. It can be reliable sources for special goods, and tidbits of information about a special subject.

"How to" can be anything from making cornhusk dolls to finding a good place for camping and hiking. It can be plans, instructions or tips on how to make something, or find a special place, or achieve a special goal. It may pertain to sports, hobbies and self-improvement. Or, it may relate directly to the hundreds of specialty publications such as skiing, decorating or writing songs.

You have imagination

Information is not limited to books and cassettes. It comes in many forms. Something you may sell for a little money and only a few pages might be plans or directions. A short piece (up to 50 pages) may be a report, manual, folio or pamphlet.

Later, if you get into multiple printing, photo illustrations, and many items to offer, you might produce brochures, catalogs, booklets or directories.

Think about what you might have to offer, and how much commitment you want to make. Maybe you want to prepare a short report, make a few photocopies and test the results. Or, maybe you are prepared for a larger project such as a book or a series of cassettes.

> **E-Z TIP**
> If you're really good at what you do, you might even start a newsletter or correspondence course, both of which can earn a great deal of money and provide ongoing income for years.

You know something special

Because your life is unique, you have knowledge and experience that is helpful to others. You have encountered and accomplished thousands of tasks that you have taught to friends, children or work associates. What's sometimes hard for another person might be easy for you, and that's why you loaned a helping hand.

It is this information, this specialized knowledge that sells at a large profit.

note

What do you have a special interest in? You probably do several unusual things well. Do you know how to make something that relatives think is great? Have you read about a specific subject for years as a pet interest? Maybe there's something that you would like to look into, find out about, and share—something that other people are looking into too.

> **E-Z TIP**
> Stuck for an idea? You can generate your own ideas. Think about what you could write about as you go through your day. You know something special at work. You may cook a delicious recipe. You may know how to fix things easily.

Look through magazine racks and bookstores for ideas. There's always something you "always wanted to know about." Try the library and the yellow pages for sources. Talk to your family and friends. Encourage yourself.

Who will buy?

Take a look in the classified ads section of your favorite magazines and tabloids. What kind of information is offered? Watch the repeats. Ads which offer the same materials month after month are winners.

You can be a winner too. You can easily produce and sell information in the form of short reports or longer booklets and make the same profit as these others.

Take a look at the price. Invest a little and write away for some of the materials similar to what you want to do. What do you like? What would you avoid?

Analyze your potential customer. What does that person expect? The same as you. You are a perfect example of your own customer. And, although you're willing to pay for special information that's inexpensive to reproduce, you expect your money's worth.

That's what makes repeat business and turns potential into real money.

You have something to say

Your enthusiasm will show. The amount of pleasure you get from the topic will come through the pages of the report. Go ahead—be creative. But, get the facts straight. Write what you know about. It must be original and unique. You should have something different to offer, something important to say, especially if you write about a well-known subject.

Preparing a manuscript is easy

After you have chosen a topic and decided on the approximate length, now what? You don't need to become a world authority on your subject, but research it.

Read several booklets or reports similar in format and subject matter. Compare the type of information and the depth of research. You might want to subscribe to the magazines pertaining to the topic (you may already). And, of course, talk to others who can give you input.

> *note* You can write. Don't be afraid—you have no one grading you. You have the ability to put ideas down on paper in a logical sequence that makes sense to other people. That's it. It is that easy.

Keep moving. You can begin writing as you research so you don't get caught in the bog of details. Prepare a basic outline or a list of the points you wish to cover, and write them out.

Can somebody help?

At any stage of the writing process you can hire somebody to help. A "ghostwriter" can prepare manuscript from your idea and outline. An editor can polish even the roughest copy into full, complete prose. Even a good typist can take rough copy, punctuate it, and make it more readable.

All of these people can be found by placing a small ad in the newspaper or from the classifieds in writers' magazines. You'd be surprised it doesn't cost that much and you won't have to agonize over the manuscript.

Tips on writing

If you can write a letter, you can write a short report. In fact, that's the best attitude—as though you're writing to a friend. Because what you offer is basically sound, friendly advice or instructions in the form of information.

> ⚠ **CAUTION** Be careful to always assume the basic intelligence of your reader—don't talk down. Although you are giving someone new information, that person may—and usually does—know a great deal about the subject.

The best writing is clear, easy to read, and follows an understandable sequence. Be careful not to meander or repeat. Each idea or separate point should have a beginning, a middle, and an end.

Use subheads to break up the blocks of writing and write short paragraphs and simple sentences. This is not a contest for best prose, but be sure to use the basic rules of grammar and punctuation.

Be sure to include helpful information, tips, or any keys to reading illustrations. Again, you don't have to be an artist to draw a simple "stick figure" picture, as long as it's clear and explains what you want to convey.

The standard manuscript form is typed, double space with side and top margins of about 1 1/2 inches and at least a one inch margin at the bottom. If you are not an expert typist or don't have an excellent quality typewriter, hire someone to complete the finished copy. It's not expensive and is absolutely necessary, since that is your product.

CAUTION You must have something to say. Reread your manuscript and scrutinize it to be sure you have something valuable to offer. That's a basic key to success in selling information.

Go slowly at first

You have your manuscript and you're ready for printing. Don't go to the expense of professional volume printing—not yet. Investigate your local "instant press" printers. Photo offset is a very inexpensive and efficient way to reproduce copies from several hundred to several thousand.

If you want to test a few dozen at first, even photocopies are reasonable in price. Since you have a clean manuscript, the copies will be clear and easy to read—a product to be proud of.

What about cassettes?

Prerecorded cassettes are an excellent way to sell information by mail. There's a large profit in these too! Drivers listen to cassettes while commuting and sales managers use them to follow up on seminars and meetings. With all the sound equipment available and in use today, recorded information is in great demand.

You'd be surprised how inexpensive it is to record and mass duplicate cassettes for your business of selling information. First, have a prepared manuscript to read from, and you get someone with a pleasant speaking voice to do the actual recording.

Because you need only the speaking quality recording tape, you can purchase cassettes in quantity at a very low price. Cassettes are available from bulk loading companies in any length to match the exact minutes of recorded information. That way there's no blank tape at the end, which is amateur and wastes money.

You can use a good tape recorder at home to record your information. It should have a clear, excellent sound, with no static or interference. Of course, be sure to eliminate background noises that detract from the recording. Remember, this is a business, and your product must be high quality. Later, when the orders roll in, you can go into a recording studio to produce the finest quality recording.

High speed duplicating services will mass produce tapes for you at a very reasonable price. Investigate quality and compare costs before you commit yourself.

Like printed matter, cassettes are easily mailed. Purchase cases to go with the cassettes that are being sent out. Later, you can even have cassette insert cards printed up to achieve a fine looking product.

How to protect yourself

CAUTION

To protect your rights against anyone else using what you publish, copyright the material. Both printed and recorded materials can be copyrighted.

Don't worry about unpublished manuscripts—they are protected against unauthorized copying. But, as soon as you send information to the public, it is in public domain unless it carries a copyright notice.

The notice may appear in one of three forms: the word "copyright," "copr.," or the symbol c. It must appear on the title page or the page immediately following the title page and include the name of the owner and the year date it was published.

Once you publish your work, send two copies with the proper applications and fees to the U.S. Government Library of Congress. This will insure the copyright.

 For information, write to the Register of Copyrights, The Library of Congress, Washington, D.C. 20559.

Running the business

The best thing about the information selling business is that it requires so little to start and maintain. You need only a small portion of your home to work in—with a work surface and a few common stationery supplies.

Do you want to use your own name or create a company name? Both have advantages that can work for you, but it's essentially what feels right. If you choose a company name, check the state laws to be sure you comply with any registration necessary.

 If you are thinking about using a post office box number instead of your own address, don't. Because of the number of mail-order frauds and the buyer's general skepticism, a street address offers a real place with a real person living there rather than a fly-by-night post box operation.

> You don't need to have a drawing for your logo—simply the first letter of your last name or the initials of the company will do. A local printer can advise you about the different type styles available for letterhead.

You'll need sharp looking letterhead stationery, envelopes and mailing labels. And, you don't have to spend a fortune for elaborate printing on high quality paper. If you have any artistic ability, you can create your own logo and type with press-on type available at art stores.

Be cautious when you order the letterhead and check the price differences before you go ahead. There is a large difference among grades of paper and added copies for using a color rather than black or for using two colors. Embossing costs more, as do special sizes of envelopes.

Stick with standard sizes and clear, standard type styles. Using a paper with a slight tint to it with black type gives the illusion of two color printing and looks smart. Photo offset printers can produce 500 to 1,000 sheets of clean printing for little cost if you supply the finished prototype.

As you get rolling in the business, you will find a high quality postal scale and meter can save you postage costs and the extra trips to the post office.

Books and printed matter can be mailed at a special postal rate. Each order should be marked: Special 4th Class Book Rate. However, for light materials, a few cents more for extra postage for first class may be worth it to fulfill a prompt response.

Selling wholesale

You don't have to publish your own writing or ideas to run a profitable information selling business. It's quite easy to make a connection with the many wholesale book companies distributing by mail. Often these wholesale booksellers can supply catalogs, or at least supply basic copy for you to make your own.

You can also distribute someone else's materials. Of course, you have to pay royalties, but there's no overhead in preparation.

Remainder lots of books are available from major publishers. Don't worry if these books didn't sell in the bookstores. HOW you market the books is as important as what is in them. These publishers usually dictate the retail cost of the books, but you can get a tidy fifty percent mark-up.

note The best way to get into selling other publications is to first establish your own list, and then offer books, reports, and catalogs of materials related in subject matter.

Just testing

Classified ads, display ads and direct mail offers are the ways to sell your information by mail. Since you haven't gone through the expense of mass producing your materials, you can gamble a little on the type of advertising you want to do.

How can you tell if your materials will sell? You run test ads, check the results, and analyze what kind of draw or appeal there is for your product. Then you analyze the response to the actual product. Were many sent back for refunds? Did you get a high percentage of orders from specific ads?

note To calculate a successful test, you need to figure the percentage of response for you to break even, to profit, and to profit greatly. Go ahead—dream. Believe it will happen—and you will profit.

note Don't get discouraged. You need persistence to continue testing and running inexpensive ads. Successful people win more often because they stay in the game.

Some of the things tested for are price, the type of publication, and the ad appeal. Successful ads in one publication can be used for another. If an ad doesn't seem to work, reword it and try again. It is only through testing that you will know your products' appeal. The actual results will give you an indication of how much of one item will sell.

Running classifieds

Have you looked at all the magazines that cater to your subject? Choose the type of publication whose readers have demonstrated the same interests as your materials offer. The product must appeal to hundreds of readers of these publications.

Check the ads for similar materials. How long have they been running? Be prepared to run your ad for months. Often a big draw doesn't happen until the second, third or fourth repeat.

CAUTION

Apply caution if you are trying for a big audience with a large distribution publication—your product might not have a mass appeal, and it may cost more to advertise in a larger circulation magazine. On the other hand, small local publications have only a limited draw for specialized information—unless it is regional.

The best way to sell your information by mail is in a two-step approach. Few items are bought directly from a short ad with a large price, but there's a high response on things for free.

Place a short, inexpensive ad in the classifieds section of the publication you choose. The ad should

Definition: If you place different ads in several magazines, or under different headings, how can you tell where the response came from? You include a code in the address. This is called keying the address.

be to the point, accurate to the type of information, and enticing. You might point out some benefit the reader would get, such as earning extra money or learning a special secret. Include a few words about "free details," or "write for free information."

DEFINITION

These ads—called *leader classifieds*—help build sound customer lists for continued returns and a solid establishment of your business.

You should always include a complete, unabbreviated name and address in the classified ad. In the company name or in the street address, you place your key that indicates in which magazine the ad was placed, and in which issue. Usually, keys come in the form of division, department or suite numbers. The easiest keys simply substitute one letter for the name of the publication and a number to indicate which month the ad appeared.

Once you get inquiries from the classified ads, you send your pitch—a printed sales letter or brochure. You can have a one-page description of your product which includes an order form, or you can be more elaborate and produce a sales package. It is this conversion—from inquiry to order—that makes you money.

Display ads

Although classified ads produce inquiries and potential buyers at a lower cost, sometimes you have a product that will sell better another way. Display ads, also called space ads, are the best way to advertise if you need to show your product.

A small line drawing of one of your products with a reasonable price and details, as well as information about a free catalog, will bring in good long-term customers.

E-Z TIP Some publications offer an additional fifteen percent discount for ads from a small mail-order business.

Buying space in publications is not difficult. Nor do you need an advertising agency to do it for you. In fact, you can save the agency discount for yourself by establishing your own in-house agency.

note Check with the publication for the *rate card*—the details of ordering space—and for the requirements of buying ad space. The advertising representative will be most helpful in teaching you how to place an ad. You can call that person, or write, if the publication is in a different city.

Direct mail

Direct mail is a tried and true way to make money in the mail-order business. But don't try it as a beginner—only if you have a sure seller and can afford the expense of printing the package.

Each direct mail package has a sales letter, a brochure, an order form, and a reply envelope.

The sales letter must be personal and have a great appearance. Have it run off on letterhead in two colors. It should discuss the benefits of the product and include a guarantee. Push for the order—ORDER NOW—stressing action.

All direct mail advertising must be tested first. A good test for a small business is 200 to 300 pieces.

The brochure should discuss the features of your product rather than appeals. It should be in color with illustrations and look professional. You don't need to provide a postage paid reply—it doesn't make a big difference.

Your own list of possible buyers from classified leaders is the best list for selling related materials. You can also rent lists from companies and get pre-addressed gummed labels. Be careful to choose lists related to your materials.

Writing ad copy

If you plan to sell something you didn't write, you should be totally familiar with the contents of the information you plan to sell. Read through or listen to the product. Why would someone want to buy it?

Good ad copy gets the reader's attention. Try out a few snappy phrases until you get one you're happy with. Arouse the reader's curiosity. What is the basic, bottom-line appeal?

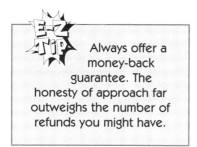

Make a list of the features and benefits. Will it show how to earn money? Will it teach something new? Will the reader learn how to do something important?

Be credible in what you're writing—don't cheat the buyer. Don't give the product benefits or features it doesn't have. When you're honest with the customer, you will get repeat business over and over.

Talk to the reader directly. Use short sentences packed with action verbs, and persuade the customer to ACT NOW, while it is at hand. Then fill in the details of the product to make it sound essential to have. Be sure to include an order form—either as part of the letter or separately.

You're successful

The fun part is when the checks come in and you complete the promises you advertised, sending the information out. There are government regulations concerning prompt responses, so be certain to ship your order within thirty days of receiving the request, or you must inform the customer of the delay and offer a full refund.

Here's where you put your organizational skills to a test. It's important to keep the inquiries and orders straight, so you're sure to send out the proper materials for each request. You might invest in a pre-inked stamp that marks the inquiry or order "received," and another stamp to mark the date it came in and the date it was responded to.

Analyzing results

Are your ads pulling? Is one magazine better than another? How many inquiries are you getting? How many convert into sales? How much money are you making?

An easy way to analyze results is to keep accurate records of the responses. You can then determine whether you want to keep renewing your classifieds, or if you need to change your sales letter.

 To make a record sheet, you can use accountants' column paper or use a ruler to make your own. You should have a separate page for each ad you placed, or for each key. The top of the sheet should have the following information: the name of the publication; the issue number or date; the date the issue was placed on sale; the address key; the size and cost of the ad; which ad you used; the price of the product; and the profit.

The columns of the record sheet should be divided into two categories— inquiries from the classified ads, and orders placed from the sales literature mailed in response to the inquiries.

Along the left side, number consecutively in a vertical column. These numbers indicate the number of dates that you received answers to your ad or orders from the sales literature.

The headings under inquiries are: date received, number received, and running total. The headings under orders should be: number of orders received, running total, cash sales, and running total for cash sales.

In order to decide if your classified ad has been a worthwhile investment, you can determine the cost per inquiry by dividing the number of inquiries into the total cost per ad. Compare three months worth of ads, and compare the average results to the ads run in another magazine. Which has provided the best response?

But, inquiries are not what you're after. Sales and profit are more important. How many orders are you getting?

You can find out the cost of advertising per order by first adding the cost of the sales literature to the cost of the ad. Then divide the total number of orders into that sum.

To figure out how much pure profit you have, simply take the running total for cash sales, subtract the cost of your product per order and the cost of mailing and handling; subtract the cost of sending the sales literature per each order and the cost of the ad.

Going to press

The test ads worked, and you get more orders in than you ever imagined. What do you do? Maybe you only had some material photocopied to see if it would be in demand, or you only prepared a few dozen cassettes for trial. Now you mass produce.

Don't be too hasty, however. Carefully calculate the amount of returns and the possible demand.

When you have a successful item, it is time to go to typesetting and printing. Local typesetters can advise you about the style and size of the type for your printed matter. Discuss it thoroughly, and be sure you know exactly the estimate of costs—it can be surprisingly expensive.

Ready to go to press? Compare prices. Get at least three comparative quotes from printers. Be sure to take a good look at the work they do. Is the type clear, is it well-aligned on the paper, nothing crooked? Is everybody clear on what is expected? Then, roll 'em.

What are the laws?

Information selling businesses are encouraged by the United States Government, but there are rules and regulations concerning the proper conduct of the business enterprise.

The most significant aspect the authorities look for is possible fraud, so you have to be careful to advertise only what you are selling. Although most advertising copy brightens the benefits and good aspects of products, be sure it in no way misleads the buyer.

You can use testimonials in ad copy and sales literature. In fact, they are an excellent way to sell. But, they must be backed up with pure fact and a person who can make the claim.

> **note** Since most states require sales tax, check with your local authorities on how to get a state tax number and collect and turn in the sales taxes.

If you have a genuine product to sell, use a direct, honest sales approach, and pay your taxes. You'll never have trouble with the law.

What to do with all this money?

Even if you never handled bookkeeping, you can keep accurate records for yourself—and the government. You can purchase a bookkeeping pad at a stationery store, or just get some accountants' 4-column paper.

List every expense related to the business. Carefully note the date, the exact amount, the type of purchase (such as stamps, photocopies), and the place of purchase. Keep all receipts. Put them in order and clip them to the page. When you have a larger volume of trade, you can file receipts according to vendor.

List all income. You will be responsible and could be audited. On a separate page or in a separate column, write down each check or money order you receive, and the source and date of the check.

Use a separate business checking account for all business transactions. This makes it clear and simple for you to analyze your profit and to keep the records separate from your personal accounts.

Building repeat business

Once you have a successful product with plenty of orders coming in, don't be tempted to expand too quickly. Carefully choose only one or two more products to add to your business, and go through all the testing steps with each one.

Even though you may feel great about the response to your first few ventures, never put all the profit back into more expensive advertising or elaborate printing. Keep some profit—reinvest only a little at a time.

Doesn't it feel great to have your own business? And, you truly haven't spent much time or money. In fact, your small investment may have already doubled or tripled. If you want to attain everything you have always dreamed of, go ahead—get started. Now.

How to sell books by mail

Now that you wrote that attractive report, how are you going to sell it? Perhaps you have already tried by placing a carefully written classified or maybe a large display ad, then waited for the postman to pile the flood of orders in your box. What happened? The odds are 100 to 1 that you came up with a couple of orders for all the time and effort. Why? You see continuous ads, small ones and full page $4,000 ads in newspapers, and magazines offering books and information. Many of them are repeated over and over again by the same advertiser. You

know that they are making it or they could not continue to advertise month after month. How are they making it when you don't seem to have any luck?

By examining the operations of these successful people we find that they use several simple and easy methods to produce excessive profits in the Mail-Order Book Selling Business. When you know these methods and put them to work you will find that you have the opportunity to make big money in this business.

 To start yourself on the road to success in writing your own books and reports then selling them...Anytime and every time you think of an idea or book title, write it down immediately. Regardless of how idiotic it may appear to you at first, it could be the ingredient you need to start you on the way to a fortune. File your notes and look them over periodically. You put yourself in a position where you have a good chance to come up with an idea or a title that will be a real money-making "blockbuster."

If your writings are about your own experiences on an inspirational or how-to subject, consider writing the book as well as the ads that sell it, in the "first person." This gives the reader the feeling he is getting personal communication and is not just a number in a computer.

Many in mail-order business have indicated that it is not a good policy and often a waste of time and money to advertise in a general daily or weekly newspaper. This is true under ordinary circumstances, but we find that when you have a real "strong" title it pays to place conservative "test" ads in the newspaper in order to learn the results quickly. However, one must keep extensive records in order to compare results and determine if they may have a winner.

note When tests indicate you have a winner, all that is left to do is expand the advertising in the proper media and fill orders.

It is advisable to structure the price of your book so an offer will stand an advertising expense of at least one-half of the selling price. You need to spend this much for advertising in order to be successful.

A 100% guarantee is a must in the book selling business. Not everyone who purchases your book, regardless of how "great" it is, is going to benefit from it. There are always a few who will want their money back. Have a unique guarantee which reassures them they haven't spent their money until they are satisfied. This can be done in many different ways, such as holding their checks for 30 days or longer before depositing them.

For the author/self-publisher, selling by mail is really the only way to go. The production costs are low because the value is in the information, not necessarily in the number of pages written. Mail-order is one of the finest businesses ever for the little guy who wants the opportunity to try for the big "bucks!" All you have to do is test with just small expenditure, correct your mistakes and let the business expand itself!

Action pictures used in your ads get fabulous results if handled right. Especially productive are ideas showing your product in action.

> **E-Z TIP**
>
> Search out the drawings and pictures used in better ads that run month after month to learn what effective copywriting is all about, then use the same ideas for your comparative publication.

If you are able to write a self improvement book or handbook with very valuable information and at the same time make it lively, witty and interesting, you could have the makings of a million dollar winner. After your first tests prove reasonable, determine if a more reasonable price structure will produce better net profit through appealing to a large audience. When you find it hitting, promote it in every way possible. Send out several hundred copies to book reviewers to get write-ups in as many publications as possible. Learn to deal with the many small booksellers and bookstores, or cooperate with some large distributors to get the books out through their normal channels.

As you grow and progress, build and maintain your name lists. Make them available to other firms who wish to make offers to proven buyers.

When you find the right combination (title, body and ad), a lot of money can be made in a short time and it is a great thrill to write an ad, test it, and see the money pouring in from your own creative ability.

Publish your book yourself, and you also control the entire operation. If it doesn't sell, you must abandon it before the heavy promotional expenditures bury you. You remain flexible and diversified when you are your own publisher.

Run some small classified advertisements in the *WallStreet Journal* and other good publications to get inquiries. When enough books are sold to more than cover the cost of the ads and mailings, slowly, as the profits build, run more and larger ads. As sales prove your publications to be winners, you can run full page ads in national magazines, inviting direct orders with a coupon included in the ads.

The large publishing companies use a shotgun approach, publishing many titles while profiting from the few successful ones. They can't begin to market effectively all the many books on their list. Trying to sell your book through them is generally futile.

Remember, as you sit down to write, the information should be about something in which you are knowledgeable and interested, or something you thoroughly researched. It must have some value for the readers and they should benefit by having read it. If it is not helpful to the reader and the benefits are not there, sales cannot be sustained.

In summary, your book must fill a genuine need; the price structure must be correct, there has to be a large or mass market for the information in your book, your advertising must be believable and offer a strong guarantee, and you must thoroughly test before investing substantial amounts to promote and sell the book.

How to sell research papers by mail

One of the easiest ways to make money in the mail-order business is to sell information research papers, or folios, to opportunity seekers. You can buy folios in large quantities at fantastic wholesale prices—or, you can let your supplier drop-ship your orders for you.

If you make direct mailings to opportunity seekers, simply enclose a few extra circulars offering folios containing valid, worthwhile money-making information and watch the orders come pouring in.

You can also run ads in large mass circulation magazines such as *Popular Mechanics, Field & Stream, Specialty Salesman* or the *The Globe*. Actually, there are dozens of newsstand publications that are ideal for research paper selling.

The most successful advertisers offer "free details." When they receive inquiries, they mail out well printed, professionally written sales material describing the research papers they are selling. If you use this method, get in the habit of answering every inquiry by RETURN MAIL. The person who wrote to you is waiting for your sales literature. Get it to him as quickly as possible!

E-Z TIP: Write your own brief, to-the-point ad, run it continuously, and you will be swamped with requests for your literature! (Incidentally, most publishers of research papers supply sales literature that you can have printed with your name and address right on it.)

To give you an idea of what kind of ads research paper dealers run, here are a few samples of ads that are currently running in large mass circulation magazines:

Establish Successful Mail-Order Business! Write!

Earn Big Profits in Your Own Mail-Order Business! Free Details!

Start your own Home Mail-Order Business. Send stamp for complete information.

You will make more money by running one ad in three issues of a publication than if you run one ad once in three different publications. Also, you should plan to make several mailings to each person who writes to you. Many people put aside your literature when they receive it, and only order when they are reminded by a follow-up mailing.

If you are new at mail-order selling, you should write to several dealers running ads like those listed above and then STUDY very carefully the literature they send you. One of the companies supplying research papers that you can sell by mail is:

Packerland Publishing Co., P.O. Box 3193, Green Bay, WI 54305

Packerland is a very reliable, well established publishing house which specializes in printing research papers for opportunity seekers. Their research papers are well-printed and offer very good information to those who purchase them.

This company will sell you titles in small wholesale quantities, so that you can ship your own orders and they also run a very efficient drop-ship service.

They also can provide you with 8 1/2 x 11 circulars which your own printer can reproduce for you. If you make direct mailings to opportunity seekers, this firm will also sell you the names of people who answered their ads in such publications as *Salesman Opportunity, Specialty Salesman, Money Making Opportunities*, etc.

They will send you FREE information on their dealer program upon request.

The Publisher's Source, 3200-10 Buford Hwy., NW, Duluth, GA 30136

The Publisher's Source stocks over 400 fast selling mail-order research papers. You can buy their titles in wholesale quantities of ten or more. And they will drop-ship orders for you, if you prefer.

This company also has 8 1/2 x 11 circulars available. They will send you camera ready copies which your own printer can reproduce for you.

The Publisher's Source also sells the names of opportunity seekers who respond to their ads in the large mass circulation magazines for a moderate price—all neatly printed on peel/stick labels in zip code order.

Martin's Mail-Order Sales, PO Box 141, Fremont, CA 94537

Martin's will supply you with 26 mail-order folios that you can sell by mail. They offer drop-shipping service, or you can buy in small wholesale lots and fill the orders yourself.

They also will supply you with camera ready circulars which your own printer can reproduce for you. Martin's will send you a free catalog upon request.

Midwest Mail Sales, Box 44Rx, Shawano, WI 54166

Midwest is a firm that handles over forty titles of interest to mail-order beginners and they will send you a complete catalog for a nominal fee. They sell shipping labels to dealers at a very reasonable price.

How to sell hobby items by mail

The first rule of
Mail-Order selling
is to sell what you yourself
would buy.

You can, if you are ambitious, start a mail-order business selling collectibles to hobbyists by mail. To begin, first find a hobby that appeals to you. Next, spend several weeks researching that hobby. Learn what collectors want and how much they are willing to pay for it. You should also know what other dealers are willing to pay for the merchandise which they sell. And, you must be willing to pay the same amounts.

Perhaps you already know exactly what you want to sell. If you have been collecting old Valentines, then start a mail-order business buying and selling old Valentines. Or stamps. Or comic books. To give you an idea of what collectors buy and sell by mail, here is a partial list of today's collectibles!

Advertising Cards	Atlases	Airplane Photos
Autographs	Arrowheads	Antique Barbed Wire
Automobile Manuals	Baseball Cards	Beer Labels
Beatles Items	Belt Buckles	Boat Photographs
Buttons	Cartoon Books	Cigar Boxes
Cigar Labels	Circus Posters	Children's Books
Coins	Comic Books	Cookbooks
Diaries	Dolls	Doll Clothes
Dog Pictures	FBI Posters	Fishing Licenses
Street Car Tokens	Fruit Jar Labels	Gems, Minerals
Greeting Cards	Gun Catalogs	Hunting Licenses
Indian Relics	License Plates	Movie Magazines

Maps	Menus	Music Boxes
Military Medals	Newspapers	Old Magazines
Old Toys	Old Pencils	Old Calendars
Old Jewelry	Paper Currency	Phonograph Records
Political Buttons	Postcards	Railroad Books
Railroad Passes	Salt/Pepper Shakers	Stock Certificates
Stamps	Sheet Music	Theatre Programs
Thimbles	Train Photos	Valentines

I suggest you send for sample copies of two magazines. They are read avidly by hobby dealers and hobby collectors alike:

The Collectors News, Box 156, Grundy Center, IA 50638

The Antique Trader Weekly, Box 1050, Dubuque, IA 52001

Each publication contains around 70 or 80 pages of ads from dealers and collectors. Almost every hobby publication, large or small, if listed within its pages.

 Once you select your field, start a file. Keep copies of all the ads selling your kind of merchandise. Also keep ads showing the dealers' buying prices. If price lists are offered in ads, send for them and study them. Make yourself an expert in your field.

Your next step is to look for merchandise in your own community. Here are some suggestions:

1.   Attending flea markets and antique shows. Don't be afraid to make inquiries of dealers. They often have what they consider "junk" stashed away, assuming that it isn't of much value to anyone. I once discovered a fabulous stamp collection that way!

2.   Browse thrift shops.

3.   Study garage sale ads in your local newspaper. Visit any that sound promising. (Sometimes, it pays to telephone. They may be able to direct you to others who have exactly what you need!)

4.   Place "Wanted to Buy" ads in your local Swapper's News or newspaper. Be sure to list your phone number.

It is amazing what you can find in your local community if you work at it. If you can't find enough merchandise locally, run ads in the Collector's Magazines. Their rates are very low. And, you will soon discover that they are widely read!

Try to locate any publication that deals with your field. Often, you can locate small mimeographed publications and newsletters which will give you all kinds of useful information.

Once you accumulate a decent stock of merchandise, you are ready to begin selling it. If there are publications specializing in your field, by all means advertise there. You have a ready-made audience! Also, run ads in the big hobby magazines.

Type a list of what you have and have a printer make a hundred or so copies for you. Hobbyists don't mind typewritten mimeographed or Xerox copies—it's half the fun of collecting. Then, run your ad. Your ad can merely offer your list to interested collectors free (or for a stamp, to weed out coupon clippers). Or, you can offer to make a sale straight from the ad. If you do the latter, stick in your price list with the merchandise. It will be read...eagerly!

Here are a few sample ads run by hobby dealers for your consideration:

"Railroad Timetables, 1940's Four Different—$4.00 postpaid."

"Old Children's Books and Texts. Stamp for List."

"85,000 Comic Books, Movie Magazines, Funnies, etc., 1900-1957. Catalog $1.00 (Refundable)."

"Original Movie Posters, Pressbooks, Stills, 1919-1975—Catalog—$.50"

"Sleigh Bells! Stamp for list."

As you progress, you will learn continually. Most hobby dealers will tell you that they learn more from the collectors who buy from them than they could ever learn from any other source.

Below are some other hobby publications that may interest you. You can write to these publications and request a sample copy. However, it is a good idea to include postage when requesting copies from the publisher.

Hobbies, 1006 S. Michigan Ave, Chicago, IL 60605

> **Definition:** Just in case you are not familiar with the phrase, "SASE" means "Self-addressed, stamped envelope."

Lynn's Weekly Stamp News, Box 29, Sidney, OH 45365

Autograph Times, 1125 W. Baseline Road, Mesa, AZ 85210

The Autograph News, 7540 S. Memorial Parkway, Huntsville, AL 35802

Doll Castle News, 37 Belvidere Ave., P.O. Box 247, Washington, NJ 07882

Western Stamp Collector, Box 10, Albany, OR 97321

Jessie's Homemaker, 731 Blue Bell St., Fort Collins, CO 80521

Coin & Stamp Trading News, Box 11101, Santa Rosa, CA 95406

Canadian Hobby Shopper, Box 3382, Halifax South, NS, Canada, B3J 3J1

Stamps Magazine, 153 Waverly Place, New York, NY 10001

Managing your promotions and ads

10

Chapter 10

Managing your promotions and ads

DEFINITION

Promotion advertising differs significantly from consumer franchise building advertising. The latter is long-term in nature and aimed at giving customers reasons to buy. Promotion advertising is short-term. It pushes for the order by providing incentives, coupons, rebates, premiums and contents.

The usual medium for promotion advertising is print. Some big-budget advertisers use broadcast (radio and television) to get consumers to look for their promotion advertising in their local newspapers.

As a rule, promotion advertising should be specific and should call only for the consumer to perform a desired action. Resist including extraneous points in the promotional ad. Focus on a simple call to action.

For example: Your ad copy may ask the readers to (1) Redeem this coupon and save $2, or (2) Buy two packs and get the third one free, or (3) Fill out coupon and enter sweepstakes to win $100,000, or (4) Buy two of the products and receive a free gift worth $10. Most promotion events are price or added-value oriented campaigns.

 Final point: Do not make your redemption procedure complicated and confusing. Avoid having more than one time offers where the consumer is forced to use math in order to determine which ones make him/her save more money.

> *note* As such, it is imperative that when writing copy, the ad should appeal more to the wallet than the emotion.

Your task is to make it easy for the consumer. Avoid making them decide. That's too much work.

How to write attention compelling advertisements

All sales begin with some form of advertising. To build sales, this advertising must be seen or heard by potential buyers, and cause them to react to the advertising in some way. The credit for the success, or the blame for the failure, of almost all ads reverts back to the ad itself.

Generally, the ad writer wants the prospect to do one of the following:

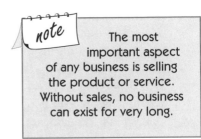

> *note* The most important aspect of any business is selling the product or service. Without sales, no business can exist for very long.

1) Visit the store to see and judge the product for himself, or immediately write a check and send for the merchandise being advertised.

2) Phone for an appointment to hear the full sales presentation, or write for further information which amounts to the same thing.

The bottom line in any ad is quite simple: To make the reader buy the product or service. Any ad that causes the reader to only pause in this thinking, to just admire the product, or to simply believe what's written about the product—is not doing its job completely.

In order to elicit the desired action from the prospect, all ads are written according to a simple master formula which is:

- attract the "attention" of your prospect

- "interest" your prospect in the product

- cause your prospect to "desire" the product

- demand "action" from the prospect

Never forget the basic rule of advertising copywriting: If the ad is not read, it won't stimulate any sale; if it is not seen, it cannot be read; and if it does not command or grab the attention of the reader, it will not be seen!

Most successful advertising copywriters know these fundamentals backwards and forwards. Whether you know them or you're just now being exposed to them, your knowledge and practice of these fundamentals determines the extent of your success as an advertising copywriter.

note The ad writer must know exactly what he wants the reader to do, and any that does not elicit the desired action is an absolute waste of time and money.

Classified ads

Classified ads are the ads from which all successful businesses are started. These small, relatively inexpensive ads, give the beginner an opportunity to advertise a product or service without losing their shirt if the ad doesn't pull or the people don't break the door down with demands for the product. Classified ads are written according to all the advertising rules. What is said in a classified ad is the same that's said in a larger, more elaborate type of ad, except in condensed form.

To start learning how to write good classified ads, clip ten classified ads from ten different mail-order type publications—ads that you think are pretty good. Paste each of these ads onto a separate sheet of paper.

Analyze each of these ads: How has the writer attracted your attention—what about the ads keeps your interest—are you stimulated to want to know more about the product being advertised—and finally, what action must you take? Are all of these points covered in the ad? How strongly are you "turned on" by each of these ads?

Rate these ads on a scale of one to ten, with ten being the best according to the formula I gave you. Now, just for practice, without clipping the ads, do the same thing with ten different ads from a Montgomery Wards or J.C. Penney's catalog. In fact, every ad you see from now on, quickly analyze it, and rate it on your scale. If you practice this exercise on a regular basis, you'll soon quickly recognize the "Power Points" of any ad you see, and know whether an ad is good, bad or otherwise, and what makes it so.

Practice for an hour each day, write the ads you've rated 8, 9 and 10 exactly as they were written. This gives you the feel of the fundamentals and style necessary in writing classified ads.

Your next project is to pick out what you consider to be the ten worst ads you can find in the classifieds sections. Clip these out and paste them onto a sheet of paper so you can work on them.

Read these ads over a couple of times, and then beside each of them, write a short comment stating why you think it's bad: Lost in the crowd, doesn't attract attention—doesn't hold the reader's interest—nothing special to make the reader want to own the product—no demand for action.

You probably already know what's coming next, and that's right. Break out those pencils, erasers and scratch paper—and start rewriting these ads to include the missing elements.

Each day for the next month, practice writing the ten best ads for an hour, just the way they were originally written. Pick out ten of the worst ads, analyze those ads, and then practice rewriting those until they measure up to doing the job they were intended to do.

Once you're satisfied that the ads you rewrote are perfect, go back to each ad and cross out the words that can be eliminated without detracting from the ad. Classified ads are almost always finalized in the style of a telegram.

EXAMPLE: I'll arrive at 2 o'clock tomorrow afternoon, the 15th. Meet me at Sardi's. All my love, Jim.

EDITED FOR SENDING: Arrive 2pm—15th—Sardi's. Love, Jim.

CLASSIFIED AD: Save on your food bills! Reduced prices on every shelf in the store! Stock up now while supplies are complete! Come on in today, to Jerry's Family Supermarkets!

EDITED FOR PUBLICATION: Save on Food! Everything bargain priced! Limited Supplies! Hurry! Jerry's Markets!

> **note** Practice, and keep at it, over and over, every day—until the formula, the idea, and the feel of this kind of ad writing becomes second nature to you. This is the ONLY WAY to gain expertise in writing good classified ads.

It takes dedicated and regular practice, but you can do it. Simply recognize and understand the basic formula—practice reading and writing the good ones—and rewriting the bad ones to make them better.

Display advertisements

DEFINITION

A *display or space ad* differs from a classified ad because it has a headline, layout, and because the style isn't telegraphic. However, the fundamentals of writing the display or space ad are exactly the same as for a classified ad. The basic difference is that you have more room in which to emphasize the "master formula."

Most successful copywriters rate the headline and/or the lead sentence of an ad as the most important part. In reality, you should do the same. After all, when your ad is surrounded by hundreds of other ads, and information or entertainment, what makes you think anyone is going to see your ad?

> ⚠️ **CAUTION** If you don't capture the attention of your reader with your headline, anything beyond is useless effort and wasted money.

The truth is, they're not going to see your ad unless you grab their attention and entice them to read what

you have to say. Your headline, or lead sentence when no headline is used, has to make it more difficult for your prospect to ignore or pass over, than to stop and read your ad.

Successful advertising headlines—in classified ads, your first three to five words serve as your headline—are written as promises, either implied or direct. The former promises to show you how to save money, make money, or attain a desired goal. The latter is a warning against something undesirable.

Example of a promise: *Are You Ready To Become A Millionaire—In Just 18 Months?*

Example of a warning: *Do You Make These Mistakes In English?*

In both examples, I posed a question as the headline. Headlines that ask a question seem to attract the reader's attention almost as surely as a moth is to a flame. Once they see the question, they just can't seem to keep from reading the rest of the ad to find out the answer.

"You'll be the envy of your friends" is another kind of reader appeal to incorporate in your headline when appropriate. The appeal has to do with basic psychology: everyone wants to be well thought of, and consequently, reads the body of your ad to find out how to gain the respect and accolades of their friends.

 Wherever and whenever possible, use colloquialisms or words not usually found in advertisements. The idea is to shock or shake readers out of their reverie and cause them to take notice of your ad. Most of the headlines you see each day, have a certain sameness with just the words rearranged. Readers may see these headlines with their eyes, but their minds fail to focus on them because there's nothing different or out of the ordinary to arrest attention.

> The best headline questions are those that challenge the reader, involve self esteem, and do not allow the reader to dismiss your question with a simple yes or no.

Example of colloquialism: *Are You Developing a POT BELLY?*

Another attention-grabber kind of headline is the comparative pricegazines headline: *Three For Only $3, Regularly $3 Each!* Still another of the "tried and proven" kind of headlines is the specific question: *Do You Suffer From These Symptoms?* And of course, if you offer a strong guarantee, you should say so in your headline: *Your Money Refunded, If You Don't Make $100,000 Your First Year.*

"How To" headlines have a very strong basic appeal, but in some instances, they're better used as book titles than advertising headlines. Another approach with a very strong reader appeal is the "who else wants in on the finer things?" The psychology here is the need of everyone to belong to a group—complete with status and prestige motivations.

Whenever, and as often as possible, use the word "you" in your headline, and throughout your copy. After all, your ad should be directed to "one" person, and the person reading your ad wants to feel that you're talking to them personally, not everyone who lives on their street.

Personalize, and be specific! You can throw the teachings of your English teacher's out the window, and the rules of "third person, singular" or whatever else tends to inhibit your writing. Whenever you sit down to write advertising copy intended to pull the orders—sell the product—you should picture yourself in a one-on-one situation and "talk" to your readers just as if you were sitting across from them at your dining room table. Say what you mean, and sell the reader on the product. Be specific. Ask if these are the things that bother them—are these the things they want—and, they are the ones you want to buy the product.

> **E-Z TIP**
> Your ad should convey the feeling of excitement and movement, but should not tire the eyes or disrupt the flow of the message you are trying to present.

The layout you devise for your ad, or the frame you build around it, should also command attention. Either make it so spectacular that it stands out like lobster at a chili dinner, or so uncommonly simple that it catches the reader's eye because of its very simplicity. It's also important that you don't get cute with a lot of unrelated graphics and artwork.

Any graphics or artwork you use should be relevant to your product, its use and/or the copy you wrote about it. Graphics should not be used as artistic touches, or to create an atmosphere. Any illustrations with your ad should compliment the selling of your product, and prove or substantiate specific points in your copy.

Once you have the reader's attention, the only way you are going to keep it is by quickly and emphatically telling the reader what your product will do for him.

Your potential buyer doesn't care in the least how long it's taken you to produce the product, how long you are in business, or how many years you spent learning your craft. The buyer wants to know specifically how they are going to benefit from the purchase of your product.

Generally, wants fall into one of the following categories: Better health, more comfort, more money, more leisure time, more popularity, greater beauty, success and/or security.

Even though you have your reader's attention, you must follow through with an enumeration of the benefits they can gain. In essence, you must reiterate the advantages, comfort and happiness they'll enjoy—as you implied in your headline.

Mentally picture your prospect—determine their wants and emotional needs—put yourself in their shoes, and ask yourself: If I were reading this ad, what are the things that would appeal to me? Write your copy to appeal to your reader's wants and emotional needs/ego cravings.

Remember, it's not the safety features that sold cars for the past 50 years—or the need of transportation—it was, and almost certainly will be the advertising writer's recognition of people's wants and emotional needs/ego cravings. Visualize your prospect, recognize his wants and satisfy them. Writing good advertising copy is nothing more or less than knowing "who" your buyers are; recognizing what they want; and then telling them how your product will fulfill each of those wants. Remember this because it's one of the vitally important keys to writing advertising copy that will do the job you intend for it to do.

The "desire" portion of your ad is where you present the facts of your product; create and justify your prospect's conviction, and cause him to demand "a piece of the action" for himself.

It's vitally necessary that you present proven facts about your product because survey results show that at least 80% of the people reading your ad—especially those reading it for the first time—tend to question its authenticity.

So, the more facts you can present in the ad, the more credible your offer. As you write this part of your ad, always remember that the more facts about the product you present, the more product you'll sell.

> **E-Z TIP** People want facts as reasons, and/or excuses for buying a product—to justify to themselves and others that they were not "taken" by a slick copywriter.

It's like the girl who wants to marry the guy her father calls a "no good bum." Her heart—her emotions—tell her yes, but she needs to nullify the seed of doubt lingering in her mind—to rationalize her decision to go on with the wedding.

In other words, the "desire" portion of your ad has to build belief and credibility in the mind of your prospect. It has to assure your prospect of their good judgement in the final decision to buy—furnish evidence of the benefits you promised—and afford a safety net in case anyone should question their decision to buy.

Once you establish a belief in this manner, logic and reasoning are used to support it. People believe what they want to believe. Your reader wants to believe your ad if they read it through this far—it is up to you to support this initial desire.

> **note** People tend to believe the things that appeal to their individual desires, fears and other emotions.

Study your product and everything about it—visualize the wants of your prospective buyers—dig up the facts. You'll almost always find plenty of facts to support the buyer's reasons for buying.

Here is where you use results of tests conducted, growing sales figures to prove increasing popularity, and user testimonials or endorsements. It's also important that you present these facts—test results, sales view, and not that of the manufacturer.

Before you end this portion of your ad and get to your demand for action, summarize everything you presented thus far. Draw a mental picture for your potential buyer. Let the reader imagine owning the product. Induce them to visualize all of the benefits you promised. Give them the keys to seeing themselves richer, enjoying luxury, having time to do whatever they would like to do, with all of their dreams fulfilled.

note

This can be handled in one or two sentences, or spelled out in a paragraph or more, but it is the absolute ingredient you must include prior to closing the sale. Study all the sales presentations you ever heard—look at every winning ad—this is the element included in all of them that actually makes the sale for you. Remember it, use it, and don't try to sell anything without it.

> *note* Plan your advertisement so it has a powerful impact upon those who are "hardest" to sell. Unlike face-to-face selling, we cannot in printed advertising come to a "trial close" in our sales talk—in order to see if those who are easier to sell will welcome the dotted line without further persuasion.

As Victor Schwab puts it so succinctly in his best selling book, *How To Write A Good Advertisement:* Every one of the fundamentals in the "master formula" is necessary. Assume you are talking to the hardest ones to sell to and that the more thoroughly your copy sells both to the hard and the easily sold, the better chance you have against the competition for the consumer's dollar. Also, you are now less dependent upon the usual completely ineffective follow through on advertising effort which takes place at the sales counter.

Ask for action! Demand the money!

Lots of ads are beautiful, almost perfectly written, and quite convincing—yet, they fail to ask for or demand action from the reader. If you want the reader to have your product, then tell them so and demand that they send money now! Unless you enjoy entertaining your prospects with your beautiful writing skills, always demand that they complete the sale now, by taking action now—by calling a telephone number and ordering, or by writing their check and rushing it to the post office.

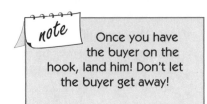
note Once you have the buyer on the hook, land him! Don't let the buyer get away!

One of the most common and best methods of moving the reader to act now is written in some form of the following:

All of this can be yours! You can start enjoying this new way of life immediately, simply by sending a check for $XX! Don't put it off, then later wish you had gotten in on the ground floor! Make out that check now, and "be IN on the ground floor!" Act now, and as an "early-bird" buyer, we'll include a big bonus package—absolutely free, simply for acting immediately! You win all the way! We take all the risk! If you are not satisfied, simply return the product and we quickly refund your money! Do it now! Get that check on its way to us today, and receive the big bonus package! After next week, we won't be able to include the bonus as a part of this fantastic deal, so act now! The sooner you act, you more you win!

Offering a reward of some kind almost always stimulates the prospect to take action. However, in mentioning the reward or bonus, be very careful that you don't end up receiving primarily requests for the bonus with mountains of requests for refunds on the product to follow. The bonus should be mentioned only casually if you are asking for product orders; and with lots of fanfare only when you are seeking inquiries.

Too often copywriters, in their enthusiasm to pull in a record number of responses, confuse the reader by "forgetting about the product," and devoting their entire space allotted for the "demand for action" to sending for the bonus. Any reward offered should be closely related to the product, and a bonus offered only for immediate action on the part of the potential buyer.

 Specify a time limit. Tell your prospect that he must act within a certain time limit or lose out on the bonus, face probably higher prices, or even the withdrawal of your offer. This is always a good hook to get action.

Any kind of guarantee you offer always helps you produce action from the prospect. Be sure you state the guarantee clearly and simply. Make it so easy to understand that even a child would not misinterpret what you are saying.

note The more liberal you can make your guarantee, the more product orders you will receive.

The action you want your prospect to take should be easy—clearly stated—and devoid of any complicated procedural steps, or numerous directions to follow.

Picture your prospects, very comfortable in their favorite easy chairs, idly flipping through a magazine while half-watching TV. They notice your ad, read through it, and are sold on your product. Now, what do they do?

Remember, they're very comfortable—you grabbed their attention, sparked interest, painted a picture of enjoying a new kind of satisfaction, and they are ready to buy.

Anything and everything you ask or cause them to do is going to disrupt this aura of comfort and contentment. Whatever they must do had better be simple, quick and easy!

Tell them without any ifs, ands or buts, what to do—*fill out the coupon, include your check for the full amount, and send it in to us today!* Make it as easy as you possibly can—simple and direct. By all means, make sure your name and address are on the order form they are supposed to complete and mail in to you—as well as just above it. People sometimes fill out a coupon, tear it off, seal it in an envelope and don't know where to send it. The easier you make it for them to respond, the more responses you'll get!

There you have it, a complete short course on how to write ads that pull more orders for you—sell more of your product for you. It's important to learn "why" ads are written as they are—to understand and use the "master formula" in your own ad writing endeavors.

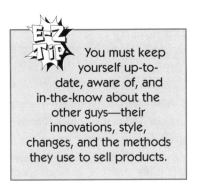

You must keep yourself up-to-date, aware of, and in-the-know about the other guys—their innovations, style, changes, and the methods they use to sell products.

By conscientiously studying good advertising copy, and practicing writing ads of your own, now that you have the knowledge to understand what makes advertising copy work, you should be able to quickly develop your copywriting abilities to produce order-pulling ads for your own products. Even so, once you do become proficient in writing ads for your own products, you must never stop "noticing" how ads are written, designed and put together by other people. To stop learning would be comparable to shutting off from the rest of the world.

The best ad writers are people in touch with the world in which they live. Every time they see a good ad, they clip it out and save it. Regularly, they review what makes them good, and why they work. There's no school in the country that can give you the same kind of education and expertise so necessary in the field of ad writing. On-the-job training—study and practice—that's what it takes—and, if you have that burning ambition to succeed, you can do it too!

Questions & answers

1) *What's the most profitable way to use classifieds?*

Classifieds are best used to build your mailing list of qualified prospects. Use classified ads to offer a free catalog, booklet or report relative to your product line.

2) *What can you sell "directly" from classifieds?*

Generally, anything and everything, so long as it doesn't cost more than $5.00 which is about the most people will pay in response to an offer in the classifieds. These types of ads are great for pulling inquiries such as: Write for further information; Send $3, get two for the price of one; Dealers wanted, send for product info and a real money-maker's kit!

3) *What are the best months of the year to advertise?*

All twelve months of the year! Responses to your ads during some months will be slower in accumulating, but by keying your ads according to the month they appear, and a careful tabulation of your returns from each keyed ad, you will see that steady year-round advertising will continue to pull orders for you, regardless of the month it's published. I've personally received inquiries and orders from ads placed as long as 2 years previous to the date of the response!

CAUTION When an ad sheet is received by someone not involved in mail-order, it is usually given a cursory glance and then discarded as "junk mail."

4) *Are mail-order publications good advertising buys?*

The least effective are the ad sheets. Most of the ads in these publications are "exchange ads," meaning that the publisher of ad sheet "A" runs the ads of publisher "B" without charge, because publisher "B" is running the ads of publisher "A" without charge. The "claimed" circulation figures of these publications are almost always based on "wishes, hopes and wants" while the "true" circulation goes out to similar small, part-time mail-order dealers.

> ⚠ **CAUTION** Ad sheets are a very poor medium for investing advertising dollars because everybody receiving a copy is a "seller" and nobody is buying.

Tabloid newspapers are slightly better than the ad sheets, but not by much! The important difference with the tabloids is in the "helpful information" articles they try to carry for the mail-order beginner. Tabloids are a "fair media" for recruiting dealers or independent sales reps for mail-order products, and for renting mailing lists, but are circulated among "sellers" with very few buyers. Besides that, the life of a mail-order tab sheet is about the same as that of your daily newspaper.

note

With mail-order magazines, it depends on the quality of the publication and its business concepts. Some mail-order magazines are nothing more than expanded ad sheets, while others—such as *Small Business Book Mart*—strive to help opportunity seekers with on-going advice and tips they can use in the development and growth of their own wealth-building projects. *Small Business Book Mart* is not just the fastest growing publication in the mail-order scene today; it's also the first publication on more than 20 years to offer real help to achieve "The American Dream" of building one's own business from a shoestring beginning into a multi-million dollar empire!

5) *How can I decide where to advertise my product?*

First of all, determine who your prospective buyers are. Then do a little market research. Talk to your friends, neighbors and people at random who might fit this profile. Ask if they would be interested in a product such as yours, and then ask which publications they read. Next, go to your public library for a listing of the publications of this type from the Standard Rate & Data Service catalogs.

Make a list of the addresses, circulation figures, reader demographics and advertising rates. To determine the true costs of your advertising and decide which is the better buy, divide the total audited circulation figure into the cost for a one inch ad: $10 per inch with a publication showing 10,000 circulation would be 10,000 into $10 or 10 per thousand. Looking at the advertising rates for *Small Business Book Mart*, you take 42,500 into $15 for an advertising rate of less than 3/10th of one cent per thousand. Obviously, your best buy in this case would be Small Business Book Mart because of the lower cost per thousand.

The more ads in the publication, the better the response the advertisers are getting, or else they wouldn't be investing their money in that publication.

Write and ask for sample copies of the magazines in which you have tentatively chosen to place your advertising. Look over their advertising. Be sure they don't or won't put your ad in the *"gutter,"* which is the inside column next to the binding. How many other mail-order type ads are they carrying? You want to go with a publication that's busy, not one that has only a few ads.

To properly test your ad, let it run through at least three consecutive issues of any publication. If your responses are small, try a different publication. Then, if your responses are still small, look at your ad and think about rewriting it for greater appeal and pulling power. In many instances, it's the ad that's at fault and not the publication's pulling power!

How to choose a print and mail dealer

A direct mail campaign is expensive! There are many ways to cut the cost of your mailings: bulk mail, SASE's, and many other ways. One of the best ways to lower your mailing costs, though, is by using a print and mail dealer.

note Print and mail dealers do exactly what their name describes. They can take your ads, usually 8 1/2 x 11 flyers, print them and mail them to names drawn from a mailing list. Their services are quite inexpensive, sometimes costing close to what your local printer would charge for printing alone.

A print & mail business runs something like this: When the dealer receives an order from a customer (for example, 1,000 8 1/2 x 11 flyers, printed and mailed), they will print the flyers on one side of the paper, with THEIR flyer on the back.

Thus, anyone who receives the customer's flyer also gets the dealer's flyer. This cuts their advertising costs. Then, they assemble a group of different orders together into one mailing. This could be as little as two pages, to as large as 50 pages. These are bulk mailed to names drawn from a mailing list, usually of opportunity seekers or mail-order enthusiasts. They could also be mailed out to those who responded to ads the print and mail dealer placed.

note The best mailing lists in mail-order are made up of people who have bought within the past 30 days. Anything over 90 days old shouldn't be used. Reputable print & mail dealers shouldn't have a problem with providing this information.

How can you be sure a print and mail dealer will do a good job for you? There are four things you should do when dealing with a print and mail dealer for the first time. The first two should be done when shopping for a dealer; the other two are done after your first order is placed.

First, send the dealer a request to be added to their mailing list. You should then receive the next mailing. If you don't want to wait for a bulk mail, send a few first-class stamps, and you'll probably receive it quicker.

Look through the mailing and observe the printing quality. Is it smudgy, smeary and hard to read, or is it crisp and clear? If the printing straight, or crooked?

Keep in mind, the quality of the mailing you receive will probably be the quality of YOUR flyer if you use this dealer. Do this for a number of dealers and you will quickly be able to determine which will give you the best print quality.

Second, find out what type of names the dealer is mailing to, and where they come from. For best results, make sure the dealers' names are fresh.

Third, when you place your printing order, request a checking copy. This is a copy of the bulk mailing, sent to you. You can then see exactly how your printing came out, the other offers surrounding yours, and your position in the mailing. Finally, also request proof of mailing. When you mail a bulk mailing at the post office, they provide you with a receipt listing the date and the number mailed. Request that a photocopy of this be mailed to you with your checking copy. Not all dealers will do this, but the reputable ones should have no problem with it.

> *note* This report is not meant to say that a lot of print & mail dealers are disreputable. Most use high quality lists and produce top notch printing. Otherwise, they would never get return customers. Just be sure that you "look before you leap."

If everything looks good, and you sent a good offer to be distributed, you should get favorable results.

22 dynamic principles of direct marketing

1) There are four important elements in a **"Direct Mail Package"** and close attention must be paid to each: (Before anything, of course, comes the essential "idea" since the conceptual strategy is still key.)

- *the graphics* (carrier) which must be opened by reader—i.e, "what does it look like?"

- *the offer:* the way the proposition is phrased—i.e "what's the deal?"

- *the copy:* the compelling description that gets the reader to buy or act—i.e. "how is it said?"

- *the list:* the targeted audience most likely willing to buy or act—i.e. "who is it sent to?"

2) **The list.** Perhaps the most important element is the list. Others believe copy is most important, but don't let ranking bother you since each element is important. Take all reasonable steps to get, use and keep the most accurate and up-to-date lists possible to increase your margin of success. Set up a system to add names and keep 'em current.

| | An excellent offer, with a striking carrier and compelling copy—if mailed to the wrong list—can be a disaster. |

3) **Heed "Daly's Law"**—"Everything takes longer and costs more!" So, it's wise to start the project in ample time to make all elements come together in an easy manner. Use "reverse timetable" to plot what needs to be done and when. For instance, you probably need to order lists first. Then, don't forget the envelopes, printed stock, other enclosures, etc. Allow time for delivery and return action plus follow-up mailings.

4) **Test.** If possible, test some or all portions of your program so you can alter methods if needed. Direct Mail is a demanding taskmaster, so if it fails it's probably you who missed somewhere, not the medium.

 5) **Heed basic principles of writing.** Compelling Direct Mail copy only seems simple, so don't be deceived. Write to a single person in simple, straightforward manner—yet with style. Long copy is not necessarily bad, in fact it can outpull short copy. Focus on main message you intend to convey.

Never forget you want action to occur...NOW. Be sure copy answers for the always-asked question: "What's in it for me?" Always keep the reader's perceived needs in mind. Do the necessary research to help determine them.

6) **Closely analyze your potential markets** and your offer so you can hone lists and copy to target your approach. Though you mail by the thousands, remember Direct Mail is more akin to a rifle than a shotgun. Write your copy to be read by one person at a time.

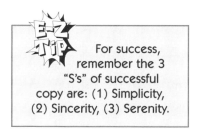 For success, remember the 3 "S's" of successful copy are: (1) Simplicity, (2) Sincerity, (3) Serenity.

7) **Remember Direct Mail is a substitute sales representative.** Where an in-person sales representative can immediately answer prospects' questions and overcome objections when raised, direct mail copy must anticipate all aspects and insure logical points are covered.

8) **Incorporate an action device**—coupon, order form, reply card or envelope, phone number—to make it easy for recipient to take desired action. Repeatedly tell recipient what action you want and make it simple to do. Put nothing in the way of getting an order or response. Use all action devices cited.

9) **A letter almost always works better** in a Direct Mail package than a package—even a catalog—without a letter. Don't worry if the letter repeats what's in the catalog, brochure or order form. It's there for a different purpose. The sales letter is a one-to-one communication to explain and sell, to get the recipient to act. The postscript is often the most-read part of the letter.

10) If all elements of the package are good, **it is imperative that repeat mailings be made.** It's difficult to wear out a good list and, unless mailings are overdone, you can't wear out your welcome. Let statistical probabilities and the laws of economics work in your favor rather than allow

difference about making frequent mailings deter you. A common error is not to mail often enough or to a wider list.

11) **Keep detailed records of everything you do.** Follow a "systems approach" so you know what happened, when and why. That way you can repeat successes and avoid failures. Sometimes the difference of a tenth of a percent or less is all it takes to turn a marginal performer into a winner.

12) **Study all elements of your package so you can know what's working.** Is it the price? The geography? The timing? The phrasing of the offer? The list? The copy? The product? Which of those myriad elements, in combination or without one element, makes the critical difference in the return? Analyze your records closely and continually until you know why you're winning and can repeat success.

> **E-Z TIP** Save, subdivide and study the good Direct Mail. You get to learn what to do—and maybe what not to do. Remember some of the things that appeal may, in fact, be "tests" that, when results are known, are failures. Never underestimate the need for simplicity and complete honesty.

13) **Keep current with changing postal rules, rates, regulations and procedures.** Regularly monitor your procedures to insure you're in full compliance.

14) **People who take actions by mail are different from those who don't.** Thus it is wise to isolate them so you can easily remail with new or different offers. Remember the axiom: "People who buy by mail...buy by mail...buy by mail..." Best lists are of mail buyers of similar products or services who recently purchased in same price range.

15) **Do what's necessary to make your mail stand out**, even "look peculiar" since it has to fight all types of competition. Clever teaser copy on outside of carrier can work wonders.

16) **Wise mail merchants work at differentiating between "suspects," "prospects," and (best of all) "customers."** Once they can distinguish names on lists among those three categories they are able to achieve cost efficiencies that novices can only dream about.

note Keep good records of what happens and when it happens with mailings to a particular list with a particular offer. Capitalize on success.

17) **Testimonials can be effective promotional tools**, especially if they're heartfelt and cogently express what the average user might feel about a product or service. They're even better when offered by celebrities or persons well-known to the audience. Treat testimonials like the jewels they are and gather more.

18) **There's no such thing as a normal percentage of return** that's universally applicable across a wide range of products and services but, over time and by keeping careful records, you can determine what some norms are for your offer (s). Your goal then is to "beat your best"...if only by 1/2 or 1/4 of a percent!

19) In producing Direct Mail programs these seven words may be cliche—but, only because they're true: **"Nothing is as simple as it seems."**

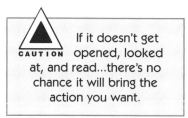

CAUTION If it doesn't get opened, looked at, and read...there's no chance it will bring the action you want.

Exercise continual care at every step of the planning and conceptual stage. Any step here can become critical if close attention isn't paid to what's happening. "To *error* is human." Yes,. I'm aware of the error, but that's the exact spelling of a sign I spotted in printer's window. I reproduce it now to emphasize how vital it is that extreme care be given to this side of production. Proofreading in a professional manner is essential.

20) Long ago I was cautioned to **be aware of these two "sinful" acronyms: KISS and CIPU**. The first, "Keep It Simple, Sweetie" describes how to tell your message, while the second cautions us to avoid lapsing into business or industrial jargon which "we" understand, but most everyone else doesn't. CIPU stands for "Clear If Previously Understood."

21) While the Power of Mail will long be with us (even though the nature of the Postal Service might change), **wise direct mailers see themselves practicing in the fields of "Direct Marketing" or "Direct Response."** They become knowledgeable of the synergistic value from use of print media (magazines, space ads, newspaper inserts, etc.) as well as electronic media (radio and/or TV) to supplement their mail promotional efforts. The combination can be powerful.

22) **Continually study and be alert to what's happening in this dynamic medium.** It may seem that not much is new, when in fact, there are subtle, but important shifts, in many of the areas delineated in each of the four elements cited in Principle #1.

Power tools for making more money

11

Chapter 11

Power tools for making more money

The mail-order catalog

Perfection in a mail-order catalog is like infinity—you can continually approach it but never quite reach it. In the case of many catalogs, however, it is not necessary to achieve perfection or even approach it very closely—in order to make the catalog vastly more profitable than it is at present. Relatively small improvements can result in a more-than-proportionate enlargement of that all-important figure on the bottom line of the financial statement.

To make as many improvements as quickly as possible is probably the most profitable procedure. Even making each new catalog a little better than the one that preceded it can produce substantial increases in sales per catalog and in total sales over a period of time.

Following are suggestions that should help your catalog do a better selling job for you. Whether you use all of them in connection with your next catalog or adopt a few at a time in the course of producing several future catalogs, the ultimate result should be very noticeable and very gratifying.

Before you create your catalog

• Look at your present catalog with extremely cold, critical and unsympathetic eyes. Pick out all the faults—large or small—that you could find if you were no longer the owner of the catalog but a nitpicking customer who was disappointed in his or her last purchase from you and is still sore about it. Such a review could be very enlightening—even if it should prove slightly embarrassing—and could make your new catalog much more profitable.

> *note* Think of your catalog as a means of helping your prospects accomplish something they want to accomplish or create an effect they want to create. Prepare your layouts, copy and illustrations accordingly.

• Put your "letterman" on your team. Review all incoming correspondence from customers and prospects during the last two years for comments, suggestions or criticisms that may be helpful in preparing your new catalog. Screen all future correspondence of this nature as it arrives and place copies of the useful letters in a special file to be reviewed before starting your next catalog.

• For each major type of product you sell, determine as many reasons as possible why different groups of prospects or customers buy or should buy this product. Arrange your groups of prospects or customers in order of importance. For each group, arrange the reasons for buying in order of their importance. Then arrange the reasons in order of importance to your total group of prospects or customers. Use the most important reasons as the basis for the copy and illustrations you use in this catalog.

If there are significant differences in the primary reasons for purchasing different types of products, make the presentation for each specific type of product fit the product, using the same type of presentation for different types of products.

Plan your catalog completely before you start preparing layouts and copy. Use all suggestions in this list as your guide for your planning.

• If the preceding reasons indicate that different appeals are needed for different groups of prospects or customers, change the wrap-around, letter or introductory page of your catalog to appeal to different groups, and separate your mailings accordingly.

• Attract new customers—reactivate dormant customers—and get bigger and better orders from present customers by adding new, exciting and extra pleasure to owning or using the types of products offered in your catalog. For example, feature dramatic new items, unusual items, items that are especially timely, etc. Include unusual facts of interest about specific items.

• Add interest to your catalog and give it a much longer life by including helpful information on how to use, operate and maintain your products—unusual uses, etc. This is information that customers can use to advantage and want to keep for future reference. Such information also increases customer confidence in your company which correspondingly increases the customer's inclination to buy from you.

note
Ring your cash register more often by using approaches in tune with the times.

• Determine whether items that were unprofitable or barely profitable in the present catalog should be promoted more vigorously in the new catalog or should be dropped and replaced by new products, Never keep an unprofitable product in your catalog just because it is one of your favorites. If it doesn't sell, get rid of it!

- Give your company a distinct personality. Promote this personality in all future catalogs to make your company not "just another mail-order marketer," but a very special marketer in the minds of your prospects and customers.

When you create your new catalog

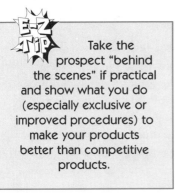

Take the prospect "behind the scenes" if practical and show what you do (especially exclusive or improved procedures) to make your products better than competitive products.

Use the following to make your prospects want your products:

♦ Write your copy to tie in with and stimulate the specific reasons for buying discussed in the preceding section.

♦ Wherever possible show your prospects how your merchandise can accomplish the results desired by the prospects to a greater degree than competitive products. Prove it by citing results of lab tests, field tests, awards received, and other special recognitions—especially testimonials and case history stories, preferably with photographs. Give the prospect every possible incentive to buy from you rather than somebody else.

♦ Put special emphasis on your products and/or services which are exclusive or markedly superior to those of your competitors—and tell your readers WHY your products and/or services are superior!

♦ Make the most of new items the first time you offer them; they are only new once. Give them every opportunity to succeed saleswise by giving them preferred position and allowing adequate space for you to do a proper educational and selling job on them at the time they are introduced.

♦ Assure prospects that is easy to use these products—that instructions are included with each order (if true) and/or are available in specific books or magazines (preferably obtainable from you). Cite case histories to prove how successful other customers were when using them.

◆ Tell prospects how to start using your merchandise properly and what other action should be taken—and when—or state that this information will be included with the shipment.

◆ If your products are bought primarily for pleasure or are considered a luxury or "non-necessity," help the prospect rationalize the value of the purchase.

Use the following procedures to make it as easy as possible for the prospect to make an accurate selection of the types of merchandise and the specific items of each type best suited for his or her purposes:

> *note* Try to group all items of the same type in the same section of your catalog.

• Arrange the groups of items in their present or potential order of importance to you profitwise. Put the most important group at the front of your catalog and the least important near the end of your catalog (but not on the last three pages).

• Within each group, arrange the individual items in descending order of quality, price, popularity or promotional possibilities.

• Give the most important items the most valuable positions and extra space for copy and illustrations. Allocate positions and space to the other items in the order of their importance.

• If practicable, use the Sears system of offering the same type of item in three different qualities—good, better and best—with different price ranges to match the differences in quality. Usually it is more effective to talk about the BEST quality first and the GOOD quality last.

• Use common copy to present features or qualities that are the same for all or most items of the same type.

• Use individual copy to talk about the features or qualities that make each specific item different from all or most of the other specific items in the group.

• In preparing the individual copy above, use "parallel construction" to help the prospect make a point-by-point comparison of the specific items as quickly, easily and accurately as possible.

Once the prospects have selected the merchandise they wish to buy, make it as easy as possible for them to order by using the next tips:

♦ Be sure your ordering information is easy to understand.

♦ Make your order form easy to use, with adequate space to write the necessary information.

note Encourage prospects to order by phone on credit, charge or c.o.d. sales and encourage them to telephone for further information they may desire.

♦ Put in one or more extra order forms to make it easier for customers to order again.

♦ Offer a 24-hour phone-in service through an arrangement with a local telephone answering service. This is especially convenient for the customer who shops in your catalog during evening or weekend hours.

Make it as easy as possible for customers to pay for their orders using the tips below:

• Offer credit card service on orders for a specified amount or more. By putting a minimum on credit card orders you will often increase the original order to at least that minimum amount. Credit card orders tend to be nearly double the size of cash orders.

• Make it easy to determine shipping charges so they can be included in cash-with-order payments.

The following should help as order starters and sales stimulators:

• Use a wrap-around letter on the front of your catalog to stimulate more orders and to do a selling job on the merchandise in the catalog; also to make special appeals to special groups or call attention to merchandise in the catalog of special interest to special groups.

Offer specials at intervals fixed throughout the catalog to entice readers to start an order. Once they buy even one lonely item, they'll tend to order other items to go with it.

• Use the wrap-around to offer order starters (loss leaders or hot items to get prospects into the catalog).

• Offer logical assortments of mixed or matched seasonal items to provide extra variety and pleasure at any given period of time. Make suggestions for these assortments and provide inducements for prospects to order them.

• Offer assortments of mixed or matched items designed for use during different seasons in order to provide variety and pleasure throughout the year (or most of it) instead of during just one season.

• Offer a free guide or plan for using each assortment above correctly and offer information on how to make the most effective overall use of the assortments.

• Offer a gift or discount for orders of certain sizes and use a stairstep graduated approach to increase the value of these discounts or gifts as the size of the order increases.

• Offer gift-shipping with gift cards.

• Provide extra services such as "Seeker Service" for items not listed in the catalog. Through extra service techniques you will make your customers more dependent on the information you provide and they will become more dedicated customers.

Stimulate promptness in ordering using the following tips:

♦ Use action incentives to spark early orders, such as premiums for ordering by a specified date; special offers for a limited time only; etc. When a time limit is involved, send a reminder (letter, promotional mailing, second catalog, etc.) timed to arrive two weeks ahead of expiration date (as nearly as you can time it with current third class mail service).

Use teaser copy and cross-references throughout the catalog to entice readers into other sections. This can be especially effective when related accessory items are sold.

♦ Mention frequently and prominently in your catalog that anyone who orders merchandise from this catalog will automatically receive the next catalog free. If you wish, this offer can be modified to require the purchase of a specified amount during the life of the catalog or by a specified date.

♦ Use the back cover of your catalog for special offers; also the inside front and back covers and the pages facing the inside covers.

♦ Concentrate service information on a Service Page; locate it on a page conveniently adjacent to the order form; and use frequent cross-references to this page throughout the catalog to stimulate extra page traffic.

♦ Humanize yourself and your catalog by making it seem like the catalog came from helpful, friendly people. If your business is truly a "family business" don't hide that fact.

◆ Watch your language! Avoid using technical "industry or business jargon" in your selling and service copy; keep legal phraseology to the absolute minimum in your guarantee.

◆ Make your entire catalog harmonious in layout and copy style, but not monotonous. Include enough variety to keep the reader interested instead of bored.

◆ Give your catalog a longer life by emphasizing the length of time that you will be able to ship from it and suggesting that readers keep the catalog for future reference.

◆ Ask for referrals from your satisfied customers; also names of friends who might like to receive a copy of the catalog. Consider testing the "cluster concept" that neighbors are very similar and mail to your customers' next door neighbors.

◆ Sell subscriptions to your catalog by providing a location on the catalog for readers to remit 50 cents for a "full year's subscription to your catalog." You can also suggest that they give a "gift subscription" to a friend very inexpensively (and thus pay for the catalog you mail to the referral).

After you create your new catalog

• Use the basic or major catalog to establish the value and regular price of the merchandise. Use other, smaller catalogs or solo mailings to promote sales from the major catalog or to provide special reasons for buying (reduced prices on individual items or special assortments, closeout, etc.).

> **note** Re-mail the same catalog to your better customers 3 to 5 weeks after you mail it the first time.

• Ask the recipient to pass the catalog along to an interested friend if the recipient already has a copy or is no longer interested in this type of merchandise.

> **note** Mail to your better customers monthly, featuring items carried in the catalog—don't rely solely on the once-or-twice-a-year catalog.

• Prepare an alternate cover for the catalog and mail the same catalog to your entire list several weeks later. You'll find it will do just about as well as the first mailing did.

• Use your catalog as a package stuffer—enclose one with every order you ship. Your best prospect is the person who just placed an order with you and received prompt and safe delivery of the items ordered.

• Be prompt in acknowledging orders (with thanks), answering inquiries, shipping merchandise and making refunds or exchanges if necessary. Remember the old adage of that great retailer Marshall Field, "the customer is always right." Less than 2% of the population will intentionally try to take advantage of you. The other 98% are well worth cultivating.

Just as every good mail-order catalog has something extra thrown in for good measure to make the customer happier, here's our extra one for good measure!

If you receive a change-of-address notice from one of your customers, immediately mail a copy of your catalog addressed to "The New Residents at (the former address of the customer)" because the new residents probably have tastes and interests very similar to your customer—after all, they bought the same house! To give this mailing added power, you might tape a note onto the front cover of the book stating that "the Smiths used our catalog regularly, maybe you'll find it equally useful."

Free printing and mailing

The biggest expenses in the field of mail-order are mailing and printing. Here is a very good, accepted plan for getting 600 3x6 circulars printed and mailed FREE!

1.   Find an offset printer in your area or by mail-order who charges $12 or $13 per thousand for printing 100 9x12's, both sides.

2.   Place the following advertisement in several leading mail-order publications:

   1,000 3x6 circulars printed for only $3. Send camera-ready copy. Our non-conflicting ad on the back. (Your name and address).

3.   On a 9x12 sheet of paper you can get six 3x6 circulars.

4.   Six orders from your advertisement nets you $18 cash.

5.   Paste your customer's camera-ready 3x6 circulars on a 9x12 sheet of paper.

6.   Paste six of your own camera-ready 3x6 circulars on another 9x12 sheet of paper. These will be printed on the reverse side of your customers' circulars.

7.   Both copies are then sent to the printer.

8.   After printing, have the printer cut each individual 3x6 circular apart.

9.   You then have six 3x6 circulars, 1,000 of each.

10.   Package the 3x6 circulars and ship them to the proper customer.

11.   Your customer has paid to have 1,000 3X6 circulars printed. They do the mailing. Your ad is printed on the back.

There it is: 6,000 3x6 circulars printed and mailed free!

Free advertising and free postage

Here is one approach you may not have recognized. There is a common thread that runs through the following books:

Hicks, Tyler G.—*Mail Order Success Secrets.*

Kameroff, Bernard—*Small-Time Operator.*

Wright, John—*The Royal Road to Riches.*

They all use their books as a means to sell you more of their products. What it amounts to is (1) a profit plus (2) free advertising plus (3) free postage for them. Hicks incorporates his "sales letter" throughout his book. Kameroff places his ads at the end of his book. Wright includes a thirteen page sales letter in his book. Therefore, when you buy their books, you pay their postage and their advertising expenses. Study their books. If you can't afford to buy them, request them at the library.

Be sure to read what I believe to be the best book on mail-order: Julian Simon, *How to Start and Operate a Mail Order Business.* Another excellent book is William Cohen's *Building a Mail Order Business.* Both are required study for the serious "mailorderphile."

If you can't afford to publish a book, try publishing a booklet and including your ads. A small booklet may consist of four 8 1/2 X 11 inch sheets folded in half and stapled, yielding a 16 page booklet. Each can be printed for about the cost of first class postage when printed in lots of a thousand.

- Start an adsheet. You can purchase space in a tabloid and have your adsheet published. Your advertisers will pay for the space, leaving you with profit, free ads and postage for you, and with relatively little work on your part!

Mail your ads when you mail your products. Your customer has already paid the postage by purchasing the product.

- Start a tabloid, magazine or catalogue. Advertisers will pay for your ads and postage.

- Look for new publications that give free ads as a promotion, then send in your ad. Request a SASE in your ad—it pays your postage and saves you time addressing envelopes.

- Start a print and mail business. Copy the pros. Mail bulk rate. Your customers will pay for your postage and printing. Simply mail your ads with theirs. Sell the names of your customers to mailing list companies.

- Start your own in-house advertising agency. You immediately save up to 17% of advertising costs. As an ad broker, profits can pay for your advertising!

How to secure a merchant account to accept VISA and MasterCard

You can seriously increase your orders by accepting credit cards as payment. It's easy and convenient for the customer, and that makes it more likely for them to order. The only problem is that it's hard for a business, especially a small mail-order business, to gain the ability to accept credit cards.

Banks are very reluctant to authorize credit card acceptance, mainly because they were burned too many times by fraudulent businesses. So, many businesses go on, accepting only checks or money orders for payment, and miss the added sales they would get through credit cards. There is a way, though, for businesses that can't get bank authorization to accept credit cards.

The easiest way to get a merchant account is to work with an Independent Sales Organization (ISO), which acts as a middleman between small businesses and banks. They charge an additional fee for each transaction, so you will pay a bit more than the standard percentage charged for credit card transactions. There will also be an application fee. Here are the typical charges to expect, as of this writing.

- Application fees: Usually, these range from $95 to $400 and may or may not be refundable.

- Point of sale terminal purchase or lease: The terminal you use to process the charge and check for fraudulent numbers is usually available from a bank for around $300. You will only be able to get this price, though,

> **note** The important thing to do is to shop around for an ISO. Get as much information as you can about each ISO you are considering, and READ it thoroughly.

if a bank authorizes you. If working through an ISO, prices will range from $400 to even as high as $1500! You can usually lease the terminal, though, at an average of $45/month. The best thing to do, though, is to find an ISO that will provide computer software that can be used in place of a terminal. This usually costs only around $150. Concerning service fees: Banks charge between 2% and 5% for processing a credit card purchase. ISO's charge higher, usually 3% to 7%. They also usually charge a per transaction fee of 20 to 25 cents, and a monthly statement fee of $5 to $10.

Why all these fees? ISO's only want to work with legitimate businesses and ones that will stay with them for a long period of time. If a business can afford these fees, they are considered less of a risk.

Look for hidden charges and unreasonable requirements. Here is a list of some of the ISO's you may want to consider. This is not an endorsement of any or all of them: these are just the most prominent ones.

- Bancard, Inc., 1233 Sherman Drive, Longmont, CO 80501 (800) 666-7575

- Data Capture Systems, 231 Quincy St., Rapid City SD 57701 (605) 341-6461

- Electronic Bankcard Systems, 2554 Lincoln Blvd., Suite 1088, Marina Del Rey, CA 90291 (213) 827-5772

- Gold Coast Bankcard Center, Ft. Lauderdale, FL (954) 492-0303

- Harbridge Merchant Services, 681 Andersen Dr., 4th Flr., Bldg. 6, Pittsburgh, PA 15220 (412) 937-1272

- Teleflora Creditline, 12233 West Olympic Blvd., Los Angeles, CA 90064 (800) 325-4849

- US Merchant Services, 775 Park Avenue, Huntington, NY 11743 (516) 427-9700

A final word: All of these services require you to fill out an application. Be 100% truthful with everything on the application and don't let the representative talk you into putting anything false down.

This would prevent you from being able to accept credit cards for an indefinite period of time. Don't let this happen to you. Most of the ISO's out there are legitimate, but there are a few that may put down spurious information, rather than lose the fees they'd receive. Be sure to look everything over twice. If you do, you'll probably find an ISO that will work with you to expand your business through the acceptance of credit cards.

> **CAUTION** If the bank affiliated with the ISO that you use found that any information on your application is false, you would probably be immediately cancelled and your business name and address would go on a "blacklist."

Build a mailing list that gets results

12

Chapter 12

Build a mailing list that gets results

Do you want to receive orders every day of the year? You can if you have a mailbox or post office box and if you sell something that people want. The "secret" is explained in this chapter so you can profit from what I learned the hard way in mail-order.

Most dealers believe that a profit cannot be made unless items with big price tags are offered to the buying public. This is far from the truth. To keep orders coming in on a regular basis you must use *good will* and *leader* items. These are good pulling offers that keep dollars coming in daily to your mailbox. In an average week leader items selling for 25 cents, 50 cents, $1.00 or postage stamps can bring in dozens and dozens of orders. Offering valuable information, for example, with price tags that build customer interest can create regular repeat buyers for your offers.

DEFINITION

For years I offered information for 50 cents, $1.00 and/or postage stamps and found that these were really big sellers that built customer trust, plus a valuable mailing list I could use over and over again.

Most of my offers are short mini-folios containing a few thousand words of helpful or money-saving information. The cost is only a few pennies to print. My profit margin is enormous even with the present cost of printing envelopes and postage. My profit margin is maintained by asking for self addressed stamped envelopes. Customers who send me 25 cents, 50 cents and $1.00 usually send larger orders later. With each out-going order, I include my other money making offers. They get a "free ride" with the original report. My repeat orders were always above 50%.

> *note* Selling information for a dollar or less may not seem like much profit to you, but you are getting valuable names of buyers for your own mailing list plus you can sell these names to other dealers for a profit.

Selling "Big Mails" is an excellent way to get your offers mailed FREE plus get valuable names you can sell to other dealers $2.00 per 100 and up.

You can get BIG response to your advertising if you just use your imagination. If you have a piece of material that has not made the rounds in mail-order publications, put the material into your own words and sell it. One dealer sells the addresses of several companies that offer wholesale mail-order printing. His ad reads as follows: *"Cheap printing! List of 50 discount printers. $1.00 and stamp"* This ad brings in 20 to 30 orders every day of the year! His profit is more than $9,000 per year from one small classified ad! You can do it too! Simply sell a good piece of information and watch the dollars roll in every day in your mailbox. This is how to keep your mailbox full of orders 365-days-a-year!

Inquiry, prospect and suspect names for your mailing list

Your lists of inquiry, prospect and suspect names are very important to the long-term success of your business. These are the names that you try to convert into loyal customers. This process can be the key to your growing business or organization.

Prospecting as an "investment" philosophy

Your customer list should be considered one of your most valuable assets. Unfortunately, customers sometimes move, die, go out of business, or just decide to take their business elsewhere. You must continue to replenish and build this list by prospecting for new customers if you want your business to grow or even just to survive.

> **Definition:**
> Prospecting—
> attempting to convert
> potential buyers into
> customers—is a means of
> investing in the future of
> your organization.

Prospecting successfully does not come easily—or inexpensively—which is why it should be considered an investment. In comparison to your results from mailings to your customers, your response from mailing to prospects will be much lower. By the time you add the costs of prospect lists, along with production costs and postage, you almost surely lose money in your attempt to recruit new customers. This loss is called *"front-end cost"* or an *"acquisition cost."*

DEFINITION

Your profit from prospecting comes on the "back-end," once you acquire these new accounts. If your new customers continue to shop from you or use your service or renew their membership to the point where your back-end profits cover your front-end costs, you've succeeded. Of course, that primarily depends on how you handle the initial contact(s) and whether you establish a good long-term relationship with the new customer.

Defining the characteristics of potential customers

Where should you look to find your potential new customers? The sources you use to develop the names of your inquiries, prospects and suspects will depend on your understanding of current customers and your business.

You want to select and maintain the names of individuals (or businesses) sharing the characteristics of your best current customers. You already know what those characteristics are. When you created your customer database, you made decisions about which data to capture for each of the customer names on the mailing list.

For example, you might determine that your best customers live in a definable geographic area or attained a certain income or gross revenue level. They may have a specific family or organizational structure. Or, they may have interests or regularly pursue activities that make them good prospects for your product or service. You want to first pursue prospects with those same characteristics.

Finding sources for prospect names

There are two different ways to build a list for prospecting:

1) Through direct prospecting (also called *one-step*).

2) Through lead generation (commonly known as *two-step*).

With a *one-step process*, you are trying to sell your product or service directly to the prospect via a list of people or firms you think are likely to DEFINITION purchase. Once the sale is closed, the prospect becomes a customer.

In a *two-step system*, first try to get prospects to indicate their interest through generating an inquiry about the product or service. You can then DEFINITION target your mailing or other sale efforts to names that have a greater likelihood of responding, and also have a certain identified need which can be fulfilled by your product or service.

There are many sources you can use to develop lists of potential customers. Here, we are going to describe some of the most productive sources for inquiry, prospect and suspect names.

Sources for inquiry names

Inquiries are people or firms that present themselves to you by asking about your product, service or organization in general. They are better potential customers than "cold" prospects or suspects because they expressed some interest in your organization and already responded in some way.

note

If you are developing a program to recruit inquiries, you must first plan how you are going to respond to the inquirer.

A list of inquiries and leads does no good unless you have a way to convert them into customers. Two factors determine how many inquiries convert to customers: (1) speed of response and (2) offer given to the inquiry. The faster you get your sales pitch into the inquirer's hands, the more likely you'll get a future order. The longer you wait, the more your results are reduced. Also, since you already invested money in this lead when generating the inquiry, make sure to present your best possible offer. The most common problem with inquiry programs is that inquirers are not treated with the care and attention they deserve.

Actively soliciting inquiries

You should not wait passively for people to inquire about your organization. You can actively invite inquiries. Below are descriptions of some of the more common ways to do this:

Media Advertising

An advertising program can stimulate inquiries about your organization in addition to selling your product or service. Your advertising program can be quite simple if you want only local exposure:

- Place classified advertisements in area newspapers.

- Buy ad space in community newsletters.

- Use a display ad for yellow pages listing.

- Purchase time on local radio or television shows.

If your audience is national, generate inquiries by:

- Placing advertisements in national magazines.

DEFINITION

- Buying space in *card decks*. A card deck is a group of promotional postcards sent to a set of defined prospects. The cards are usually wrapped in plastic, may offer products or information, and always include a way for the prospect to respond.

Whether using your advertising to sell a product or service or simply to urge people to inquire about the organization (or a combination of both), always include some way for them to respond. Coupons, a tear-off card and a

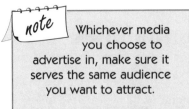

note Whichever media you choose to advertise in, make sure it serves the same audience you want to attract.

toll-free telephone number are often used to make it easy to inquire. Also, the advertisement should always feature your organization name, address and phone number prominently.

A word of caution about the method through which inquiries can respond. If you make it too easy to respond, you may get inquiries from people with no interest in your organization, but who simply like to fill out forms and/or receive mail.

It costs money to respond to inquiries (especially if these are leads for salespeople), so make sure your objectives are clear before designing your program. Are you looking to obtain as many names as possible or do you want to receive inquiries from "highly qualified" leads only?

 There are a number of ways to qualify inquiries. Roughly speaking, the more difficult (or expensive) it is to respond, the more likely it is that the inquiry has a true interest in your organization. For example:

- A few short questions on the response form may deter people who aren't really interested in your organization. In any case, YOU can qualify inquiries based on the information given and choose to add them to the list or not.

- A toll-free telephone number may produce a greater proportion of "non-qualified" responses than would a phone call for which the inquirer must pay. (The same principle holds true for postage paid vs. unstamped response form.)

Trade show exhibiting:

Companies exhibit at trade shows for a number of reasons: to sell a product, to talk to customers, to build name identification, etc.However, one benefit of trade show exhibiting which is often ignored is to talk to prospective customers and collect their names for follow-up with future mailings.

If you want to exhibit at trade shows solely for the purpose of generating leads, first answer the following questions:

- ◆ What is the expense involved in exhibiting? Registration fee? Materials for the booth? Travel costs?

- ◆ Does the type of business or individual who fits your customer profile attend?

- How many businesses or individuals attend?

- What response rates would you need to pay for the costs of exhibiting?

- Is your product or service appropriate for the show?

- Are there other benefits to exhibiting at the show, such as selling products, increasing awareness of your organization, creating goodwill, or gathering information about the competitors?

 note If you decide to exhibit at a trade show, you should have a well thought out method for collecting qualified prospect names.

Too many trade show exhibitors overlook this necessary step. At the trade show, you will want to capture the names of the visitors to your booth. As we mentioned, you also want them to give enough information about themselves to decide if they are truly qualified inquiries.

Some ways to encourage people to give the information you want include asking them to drop their business cards into a "fish bowl" or fill out a brief form. Any of these methods can be used in a raffle format (where a winning card or form is chosen to receive a prize). You must weigh the cost of running a contest against the benefit of increased response and the potential of less qualified leads.

Leads from suppliers:

Some suppliers may do lead generating publication advertising for their products or services. Typically, they turn over the inquiries to dealers for follow-up.

Seminar and meeting attendees

Giving a presentation at a seminar or meeting is a good way to make people aware of your organization. Many of them will ask for additional information about the product or service, if given the opportunity by means of a card on their seat or a tear-off portion of a handout. Of course, the registration list itself is a good source of names.

> **E-Z TIP** All organization written materials should include an invitation to contact you for further information.

Visitor Cards

Have any visitor to your business or organization fill out a card.

"Take-ones"

DEFINITION

Take-ones are small pads or forms that are attached to advertisements found on buses, public bulletin boards or kiosks. These forms include an invitation to request more information about a company's products or services.

Advertising specialties:

These are useful items (such as pens, lighters, magnets, etc.) with a company's name, slogan, address, telephone number imprinted on them.

Sources for prospect names

There are so many sources for prospect names that it is necessary to be very clear about what types of names are most appropriate for your organization. Understanding the characteristics of your best customers is vital.

Understanding your target customers can help you identify the best sources for new prospects and suspects in another way. You may decide to use one of the database fields to track how current customers heard about your business or organization. The information in this field would give an indication of where to look for potential customers.

> **note** When contacting the referral name, results will be better if you indicate who referred them to you.

Below are some of the sources for prospect and suspect names that many organizations find productive:

Referrals

Present customers may be willing to suggest the names of their friends or associates who could benefit from your product or service. These names are usually more valuable than "cold" prospects because they were selected by people who know, and are satisfied with, your organization. Similarly, the prospect will probably be receptive to (at least) listening to your offer. A recommendation coming from a friend or associate carries with it a great deal of credibility and trust.

In addition to referrals, directories and public lists are another source for prospect and suspect names. They are less valuable than referrals because they were not given to you by someone familiar with your business or organization.

> **note** Because people or even businesses are so mobile and because it takes so long to compile and print a directory, most directories have a relatively high "error" rate.

Directories and public lists

Many organizations publish directories which can be used to construct your own list of prospects. When you add the names from a directory to your own mailing list, they are usually yours to use without any restriction. Some directories do have limitations, so check before using names.

The significant amount of time needed is one of the biggest drawbacks to manually compiling a list from directories. For example, consider the time it would take to type all (or even some) of the entries in the yellow pages. In many cases, this work has already been done by a professional list compiler, who then offers the list for rent.

Here are a few of the many directories you might want to consult:

- Telephone directories—Both yellow and white pages.

- City directories or reverse directories—Organized by street and address.

- Business directories—Directories compiled by type of business.

- Association directories—Many associations publish directories with listings of their members.

- *The Directory of Directories,* published annually by The Gale Group, 835 Penobscot Building, Detroit, Michigan 48226-4094, or call toll-free 1-800-347-4253, 1-800-444-0799. Contains listings for over 9,600 organization and business directories.

- Government directories—The federal government and most state governments publish directories of their agency offices and personnel. Federal directories are available at low costs through the Superintendent of Documents, Washington, D.C. 20402.

Other lists are available through public sources:

- ◆ Local governments maintain a number of different lists which may be available in your area. Contact your city or county clerk for lists compiled from any of the following sources:

    - ◆ voter registrations

- marriage licenses

- birth certificates

- business licenses

- business loan information (also at state level)

Try association and church lists—many local organizations (such as Kiwanis or Chamber of Commerce) have lists of their members. Also, your church or synagogue's list of its members could be useful.

- hunting or fishing licenses

- fund-raisers for elected offices

- institutional lists—public schools and hospitals may also have lists of students or births

Visitor lists or customer registration forms

Many organizations use a registration device to develop lists of people who visit their facilities or participate in their programs. Retail stores in particular are known for using this technique. To build a prospect list, they invite each visitor to the store to fill out a card with his/her name and address along with any other information desired. This request for information is sometimes presented as an entry to a raffle or sweepstakes.

The main thing to keep in mind is that these are many lists that are easily and inexpensively available to you, particularly if your product or service has a wide appeal within a local area.

Other options for obtaining prospect and suspect lists

When you develop prospect and suspect lists yourself, using the above sources, the names belong to you. However, compiling lists from these sources can be very time-consuming, since much of the work is manual. You may be severely limited in the number of names compiled because of the time it takes. That time restriction might also mean that when you finally complete the list, many names have moved or are no longer appropriate to mail. Also, working on your own, you may overlook (among the thousands of list sources available) those that are best for your purposes.

> *note*
> Lists can be rented for one-time use only, unless otherwise agreed upon.

Several options are available to you for expanding your prospect list on a larger scale and without manually compiling the names. For example, rent or purchase names or exchange names with another organization:

List rental

List rental can cost anywhere from $25 to more than $100 for 1,000 names. The charge is usually higher if you want to make selections within the list (for example, by business type, last order amount, etc.). Typically, 5,000 names are a minimum order quantity. However, fewer names may be rented, depending on the total size of the list.

List owners usually include decoy names on the list to monitor the use of their lists and detect unauthorized mailings. Decoys are names that are unique to their owner's list and to each mailing. They may be

> *note*
> List purchase can be a welcome option if you determine that you want to contact the names on a multiple, or unlimited, basis.

"doctored" (or entirely phony) names, but they do have actual addresses. These decoys then inform the list owner when they receive a mailing with the "fake" name.

> *note* By exchanging lists you avoid the costs of list rental or list purchase. Of course, you must always take care to verify that the list you are getting is accurate, current and free of duplicates.

List purchase

List purchase is not as common as rental. List purchase is actually more like "long-term rental." The list is sold for permanent or long term use; that is, for some period longer than six months. The time period is usually negotiable.

If you buy a list, you must maintain it. In other words, you are responsible for updating names and addresses as needed, reviewing for and eliminating duplicates, and generally keeping the list in its most efficient mailable form.

List exchange

As the in-house list of customers, inquiries and inactive customers grows, you may be able to exchange it with other list owners for their lists. Arrange list exchanges with organizations that have similar audiences, but do not compete directly with you. Occasionally, competitors do exchange lists for offers of a non-competitive nature.

Common types of lists available for rental, purchase or exchange

Following are examples of some of the common terms used to describe available lists:

Compiled lists

Compiled lists are prepared from names found in directories and other sources of printed (usually public) information. They are "put together" based on certain predetermined criteria such as type of business or location. When you rent a compiled list, the manual work of building a list is done for you.

Another advantage of using a compiled list is that compilers often include additional data with the list. You can often select compiled lists by such variables as age and income on a consumer list and business type and number of employees on a business list.

 The disadvantages of using a compiled list are basically two-fold. You don't know how recently the list was compiled. Given the length of time it takes to compile and issue a list, the names and data could be 1 1/2 to 2 years old by the time you order and attempt to mail the list.

Also, with the exception of the possible demographic information you have about the names on the list, you have very little knowledge about whether this name has any likelihood of wanting your product or service.

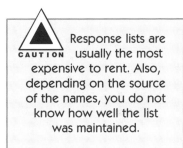
Response lists are usually the most expensive to rent. Also, depending on the source of the names, you do not know how well the list was maintained.

Subscription lists

Subscription lists are made up of people who subscribe to a publication or a service. It is important to distinguish between paid and free subscriptions when evaluating these lists for your purposes. People who paid for a subscription are considered to be better potential responders than those who request and receive a free subscription. Subscribers might not have the same propensity to buy by mail as do names on a response list. However, based on the publications they subscribe to you know more about the names (and their interests) than you do with a compiled list.

Response lists

The names on a response list already responded to some sort of offer (from another organization) and are thus considered more valuable. The theory is if they responded once, they are more likely to do so again!

Below are terms commonly used to describe the names within a list:

- **Buyers:** People who made a purchase at some time.

- **Active Buyers:** Individuals on a list who more recently (usually within the last 12 months) demonstrated some form of action, e.g. purchase, rent, subscribe to a service, etc.

- **Hotline Names:** The most recent names added to a list. These names should not be older than three months and might be able to be selected by categories as recent as 30 or 60 days. If this selection is available on a list (usually at an additional charge), it is wise to consider testing it since these individuals recently demonstrated some action and their address is probably correct.

- **Inactive Buyers:** Those who purchased, but not within the last 12 months. Be careful here: These names age. Unless the list has been cleaned recently, you may get many obsolete addresses.

- **Multibuyers:** Individuals who made more than one purchase. Multibuyers, if available on a list, are the best selection to make when renting a list.

- **Inquiries:** Names who inquired, but not yet purchased. The ages of these names are very important.

Data cards

Data cards provide basic information about rental lists.

- The price of renting or purchasing the list

- The number of names available

- The different list segments available

- Hotline names available monthly or quarterly

- List selections (and the costs of those selections) for better targeting. Typical selections include:

  - Sex

  - Geographical (by state or zip code)

  - Home vs. business address (often differentiated by whether the address has three or four lines)

  - Type of business (SIC code)

  - "Nth" name to ensure randomness for a test mailing

  - Specific name/title within the business to get the mailing (particularly if mailing to larger businesses)

- Minimum order size

- Date data card was updated

- Written description of the list

- Terms of renting or purchasing list

- Formats (and changes) for how the list is available, e.g. computer tape, microcomputer disk, Cheshire labels, peel-off labels

◆. Profile of the list, usually including the following:

- Average order size (unit of sale)

- Sex (% male, % female)

- Source of names (direct mail, membership, publication advertising, telemarketing, television and radio advertising)

- Method of payment (% cash buyers, % credit card buyers on the list)

◆ Name and address of the list manager or broker

Where to go to rent, purchase or exchange lists

There are list professionals available to help you carry out the transactions described above. In addition to handling the details of each arrangement, some may be able to advise you on which list(s) will be most effective for your purposes. Two types of list professionals—list compilers and list brokers—are described below:

List compilers

List compilers offer catalogs of the lists they built, using many of the same sources we presented above. The lists may be either compiled or response lists. The list compiler not only builds, but must maintain, the lists as well.

note It may ultimately be more efficient to use an "expert" who has already built the list you want, as long as you are prepared to purchase the names in volume.

List compilers offer literally thousands of business lists and consumer lists. The consumers on the lists range from purchasers of home burglar alarms to people who traveled to Hawaii in the past three months to businesspeople in California. New lists are made available regularly and are promoted through announcements and advertisements in direct marketing industry publications.

If compiled lists are appropriate for you, there are a number of sources for obtaining them. If you are seeking lists that are national in scope, two good places to begin your search are the:

- "Direct Mail Directory" found near the back of every issue of *Direct Marketing News,* Source Directory, 100 Avenue of the Americas, New York, NY 10013, (212) 925-7300

- Mailing List Compilers section of *Direct Mail List Rates and Data,* published by Standard Rate and Data Service, 5201 Old Orchard Road, Skokie, IL 60077.

List brokers

List brokers are the direct marketing field's mailing list specialists. They are independent agents whose primary function is to arrange the rental transaction between list users and list owners and compilers. List brokers must keep up-to-date with what is happening in the field in order to recommend the best selection of lists to achieve their clients' (the users) objectives.

The broker is paid a commission by the list owner. That commission is typically 20 percent of the list price. The broker collects the full amount of the list rental fees, deducts his commission and gives the balance to the list owner.

Some clients use brokers simply to order the lists. Others tap the broker's know-how about maintaining lists, keeping direct mail records and testing, as well as the creative aspects of direct marketing.

Full service agency

Another source to go to for arranging a mailing list transaction is the full service agency, which can provide the entire range of mailing function necessary to conduct a program. The agency can help select names, design and produce the mailing package, and carry out or arrange for the physical mailing. They can also arrange to have the orders filled, if necessary.

> *note* From free-lancers to direct response advertising agencies through full service advertising agencies, every imaginable service is available.

For a list of full service agencies, contact your local direct marketing associations or clubs, or consult the yellow pages under "Advertising—Direct Mail."

How to order a mailing list

The steps involved in ordering a mailing list may vary depending on the source used and the type of list you want to obtain. Here are some general guidelines that apply to most situations:

- Plan your list selections well in advance of a mailing. Allow at least two to four weeks for ordering and delivery of the names, as well as time for the list owner to approve the order.

- Be specific about the selections. All instructions should be written and complete.

- Specify the format you want to receive the names—computer tape, microcomputer disk, peel-off labels, hard copy, etc.

- Communicate the mailing date. If you foresee a problem in meeting it, let the list broker know as soon as possible. Also, determine whether the lists are to be delivered to you or the mailer. Specifically indicate all dates when and places where the list or computer tapes need to be delivered for each step in the processing of your mailing.

- Work closely from the start with all parties involved in the list transaction.

For additional information about these options: A good source to contact to find out more about list transactions is the Direct Marketing Association (DMA). The Direct Marketing Association is the national trade association representing both direct marketing users (such as mail-order businesses, charitable organization, and financial institutions) and suppliers (such as list professionals, advertising agencies and printers).

The Direct Marketing Association offers a wide range of services, seminars, reference books and directories on all aspects of direct marketing. For more information about the Direct Marketing Association, contact its headquarters at 1120 Avenue of the Americas, New York, NY 10036-6700 (Phone: 212-768-7277).

Successful promotion to inquiry, prospect and suspect lists is the key to keeping the current customer list growing and productive. This report has outlined the various avenues available to you in the search for these potential customer lists. Your organization may want to handle the whole effort in-house. Or, you may want to use the services of direct mail industry professionals for some or all of the steps.

Where to find the database for your customer mailing list

In-house sources

Before you think about a list of prospective customer names, you should first create a database for current customers' names and develop a mailing list.

(Remember, your current customers are most likely to respond to your future offers.)

Finding the data to include on the customer portion of your mailing list can be fairly straightforward if you have your own in-house records. Even then you may have to develop more sources to obtain additional data about your customers.

Here are some of the in-house records you can use to develop your customer database:

• **Sales Receipts/Invoices/Order Forms:** These documents can give you the following information: date of last purchase, dates of all purchases over a period of time, and amount of money spent with you. You may also be able to determine what products/services were

> ⚠️ **CAUTION** Especially if your customers are businesses, they may use two addresses. One is the "Ship-to" address, where ordered items are sent. The other is the "Bill-to" or "Mail-to" address, where invoices and catalogs are sent. Make sure you're using the correct address every time you correspond with the customer.

ordered from you. When using invoices to compile your customer list, be aware that in businesses they may be addressed to the Accounting Department rather than the individual/title most likely to purchase from you.

• **Shipping Records:** Shipping records can be an important source of customer names, particularly if your product is sold through a dealer or distributor, and you don't have direct access to customer order forms. Again, be aware that some customers may have different billing and shipping addresses.

• **Membership Lists:** Every organization is sure to have a list of its members. If your organization has several membership categories, this information should be associated with the member name when you add it to your list.

• **Registration Forms:** If your organization does not maintain a membership list, you may still be able to identify your customers from the registration forms and sign-in sheets you use at your events. One approach to collecting names is to ask attendees to add their names to your mailing list.

• **Contest Entries:** The entry forms for a sweepstakes, contest, or raffle can be used effectively to get the names of your customers. This approach might be most useful if your organization lacks customer records because you provide your product or service free of charge.

Other sources

Sometimes, your own records don't hold enough information about your customers or members. You may have to rely on other sources to capture additional database information:

♦ **Warranty Cards:** Warranty cards included in packages of merchandise can be an effective way to gather information about customers. On the card, you can request that the customer complete the demographic information and return it when he/she registers the product.

♦ **Surveys:** Phone or mail surveys are another way to gather (and later update) information on your customer database.

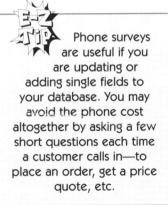

Phone surveys are useful if you are updating or adding single fields to your database. You may avoid the phone cost altogether by asking a few short questions each time a customer calls in—to place an order, get a price quote, etc.

Phone surveys can be used in a number of different ways to collect database information. For example, you can call customers and administer full questionnaires to gather complete information about them. This can be a very costly way to collect data—especially for a large number of customers. Mail surveys (which will be discussed later) may be a better technique for this type of database information collection.

Mail questionnaires can reach a larger number of customers at a lower cost than phone surveys. Mail questionnaires can be sent individually to customers. However, to save postage costs, surveys can also be inserted in mailings, included in packages of merchandise, or printed on any other correspondence with customers, such as invoices.

> **CAUTION** When you're dealing with the government, expect to go through several people to finally get to talk with someone knowledgeable about the lists that are available. This is even more of a problem when dealing with the federal government.

If you have a store or office, you can also conduct surveys by having customers fill out questionnaire cards when they visit.

Other sources you can use to build your list include:

- point-of-purchase questionnaires
- membership application forms
- questions on purchase orders, statements, invoices

At the end of this report are examples of a warranty card and a survey used to collect database information.

Your customer names are the core of your mailing list. This report has described some sources for collecting database information on current customers. You should consider every contact with a customer a potential source for collecting such information. After you collect this information, you need ways to initially get it into your database and then to regularly make sure it's current and accurate. (Out-of-date, inaccurate mailing lists waste money and reduce results.) Please see Report 3506 for some suggestions.

Get free mailing lists from federal and state governments

If you want to make money in the mailing list business, you should contact the state and federal government for sources of lists. What's available? You wouldn't believe it!

From many states you can get lists of licensed attorneys, accountants, real estate agents, veterinarians, barbers, insurance companies, architects, CPAs, nursing homes, cosmetologists, social workers, dentists, librarians, psychologists, manufacturers, licensed drivers, businesses, doctors, foreign corporations registered in the state, and many others. There are even 28 states that allow access to driver's license records!

 Be persistent. If you believe a particular list is available from the government, don't take "no" for an answer when someone says there isn't such a list.

Here are a few sources to speed you on your way:

- **FSS Surplus Personal Property Zone.** This is a list of people who bought auctioned government property from the federal government. It's broken down into several files (regions). An example: region 8-10 consisting of 38,000 buyer addresses. It's available on tape from the General Services Administration for a fee.

- **Domestic mail manual.** 8,700 paid subscribers to the government's publication on postal regulations. It's available from the government printing office.

- **Catalog of United States government publications subscriber list.** 1,400 paid subscribers to this publication which lists monthly government publications. The list is available from the Government Printing Office. Call or write for current price and format.

- **Business America,** international trade subscribers list of nearly 5,000 names and addresses of people either in export related fields, or expressing an interest. The list is available from the government printing office.

These are just a few of the many, many lists available. Some are free. Most carry a nominal charge. Be sure to specify printed directory, diskettes, or tape format. It is also advisable to inquire and make sure the file you want has the complete name and address for it to be usable—many files may only have a name and no address.

Compile, maintain and sell "red hot" name lists

13

Chapter 13

Compile, maintain and sell "red hot" name lists

The mailing list

Virtually every inquiry or buyer's name ultimately ends up on a mailing list. Some are small lists, while others contain millions of names. Some are meticulously maintained, while others are carelessly handled.

> **note**
> For those interested in mail-order advertising, mailing lists can prove to be very valuable as well as a saleable commodity.

If you wish to increase your sales, it is often a good idea to go into direct mail. To do this you begin by renting another firm's mailing lists. Or, you rent your list of customers' names to another firm. Either way, mailing lists play an important part in the everyday world of mail-order.

Basically, there are three types of lists. They are:

- house lists

- mail response lists

- compiled lists

House lists

DEFINITION

A *house list* is a list of your own customers. They may be active or inactive. They may be inquiries or buyers. They may have made ten purchases or just one, or in the case of inquiries, none. They may have placed an order in the last four months, or in the last four years. They may have spent a great deal of money or a small amount. They may be credit card buyers or cash buyers.

> **note** You can spend a great deal of money to rent outside lists, but none will bring you the financial rewards you will reap from your own customer list.

Your house list contains your most valuable asset—the names of your own customers. These are the people who purchased from you in the past and are likely to purchase from you in the future. These people know and trust you, and will order on a continuing basis.

Mail response lists

DEFINITION

Second in importance are *mail response* lists. These are people who responded to another firm's direct mail offer. The idea is to pick out a list of customers who ordered products similar to those sold by your firm. Since it is a well-known fact that these people previously responded to an offer similar to yours, there is an excellent chance that they will also respond favorably to your offer.

Compiled lists

Although the people on compiled lists do not usually respond as well as the people on house lists or mail response lists, these lists can still be helpful if properly used. These lists are not generally used by small or medium sized business firms because they are too general in nature. But large firms, such as oil companies and insurance firms, find them useful and even profitable.

I never used a compiled list and do not recommend their use for anyone but the largest mailers.

While there are no set rules that can be applied to mailing lists, here are few "rules of thumb" that can be regarded as reliable in most cases. They may not apply to your list situation, but they give you food for thought.

- The average list changes at least 15%-20% each year. Some mailing lists change only 10%, while others have as high as a 100% rate of turnover. (Lists of high school seniors, etc.)

- A direct response list (people who already purchased goods through the mail) will out-pull a compiled list.

- A customer list will out-pull all other outside lists (direct response or compiled lists).

- Allocate 10% or more of your direct mail budget to list development and maintenance. The 10% figure is the minimum amount you should spend. Most successful businesses find the more they spend the more they prosper.

- People over 35 years of age as a group respond to mail-order offers at a much higher rate than do younger people.

- People living in rural areas respond to mail-order offers at a higher rate than do people who live in urban areas.

- People who ordered through the mail within the last 3 - 6 months ("hot-line" buyers) are the most productive names you can get.

- Multiple buyers (people who made two or more separate purchases through the mail within a season) will always outpull buyers who purchased only once within a season.

- The results you can expect will vary by season and/or months of the year, and by regional areas and states.

- Every list should be checked and cleaned at least twice a year or more. It is a good idea to review and update your list at least every six months whenever possible.

> **E-Z TIP** Use outside consultants and service organizations to help you with your list decision. These people made it their business to study and understand lists.

Responsibility for maintaining and updating of your list should be delegated to a single individual whenever possible. You've heard the expression "too many cooks spoil the broth." Well, when it comes to mailing lists, it is a good idea to limit the number of individuals who handle the list to as few as is possible. The fewer the better.

Should you use lists?

The first thing to consider when trying to make a decision about a particular list is whether or not the people on that list would be interested in your product. You want a list of people that purchased something similar to your product, or at least something in the same general category. People who already purchased cheese products are perfect for you if you are selling cheese products. But, if you are selling fishing supplies you would never want to rent a list of buyers interested in cheese products. Instead, you would want to rent a list of people interested in fishing. You might consider renting a list of names from a publisher that publishes a fishing magazine. Or maybe, a list of people who recently applied for a fishing license.

What to spend

Today, there are thousands of mailing lists available in thousands of categories. Almost any offer, no matter how unusual, can be matched to an appropriate list. The price of a mailing list can start from as low as $15 per thousand to as high as $75 per thousand and more. A few of the factors that determine the price of a mailing list are:

- freshness of list
- buyer or inquiry
- amount of purchase
- multiple or one time buyer
- "hot-line" buyers
- credit card buyers
- frequency of purchase
- brokers recommend its use

When renting lists, it is imperative to find a list that parallels as closely as possible your own list of customers. The right list usually makes a tremendous difference in the results you can expect.

As you can see, many factors come into play when pricing a mailing list. The more desirable the list, the more you can expect to pay.

List brokers and compilers

It is the list broker's job to bring together the owner of a list and the firm who wishes to rent that particular list. The fee for this service is usually a flat 20% on each rental. You can rent names through a list broker for the same price you would pay on your own. So, it is to your benefit to take advantage of this service. It is to the broker's advantage to help you choose the best list available for your needs, so that if your initial test proves successful, there is a good chance you will wish to rent the whole list in the future.

note It is almost impossible to succeed in direct marketing without the help and guidance of competent list brokers and compilers.

After a list broker arranges the rental, he next bills the firm renting the list and forwards the proper payment to the owner of the lists. These services are all included in his fees.

A list compiler represents those lists owned and maintained by the company that employs him. They are specialists for the compiled list they represent. Basically, the compiler offers the same services as a broker.

Name lists—a profit center for you

note Many companies with as few as a few thousand names are earning a substantial income from the rental of their list. Larger firms who have lists in excess of 50,000 names are reaping huge rewards. If you simply bear in mind the fact that these small companies with small lists are able to gross $40,000 a year and more in rental income fees alone, you begin to grasp a measure of the significance of just how profitable the buying and selling of names can be for you. It is truly a profit center without parallel in the mail-order industry.

List prices depend on the time and money you spend compiling them. Some lists are easily accessible and you cannot charge a great deal for them.

Other lists require a great deal of time and money to compile. These lists are usually very expensive.

You have probably seen many dealers advertising their lists at cut-rate prices. In most cases these lists are worthless or so out-of-date that they are no longer of any use to anyone, except to sell to unsuspecting mail-order buyers. Try to stay away from these dealers. Most of them are selling garbage.

Your own list

Once you get your mail-order business off the ground and have a large enough list of inquiries or buyers, or both, it is a good idea to put your customer list up for rental with as many brokers as possible.

While it is true that the primary purpose of compiling your own list of customers is to generate sales of your own products, an important secondary source of income can be generated through the rental of your list to non-competing firms. Profits from the rental of house lists can be enormous. Indeed, if it were not for the monies received from list rentals, many a mail-order firm would soon be forced to go out of business.

> *note*
> It is not uncommon for many mail-order businesses to make more money from the rental of their lists than they earn from the rest of their business.

For example, let us assume that you have a customer list of 50,000 names. This list is considered small by most experts, but it still accounts for hefty revenues. If you charge $40 per thousand names, you receive $2,000 each time you rent your list. Of course, you have to allow for the brokers commission of 20% or $400. That still leaves you with $1,600, assuming there are no other costs involved. If you rent your list ten times during the course of a year you should net approximately $16,000.

Another benefit of renting your list to non-competing firms is that you are able to get new ideas and insights about what your customers' likes and

> **note** Some firms take a middle-of-the-road approach to the renting of their list. These firms make sure they rent only their old subscribers list or inactive customer list. They do not rent their current subscribers list or the names of their active customers.

dislikes are. In addition, one of the firms that rents your list may try an approach that you might want to imitate.

Many firms refuse to rent their house list to another firm. They feel that the results of their future mailings will be diluted if their customers are deluged with offers from other companies. Other firms feel just the opposite is true. They state that as long as they rent their list to a non-competing firm no harm is done. In fact, many feel that by renting their list to other companies, they are helping to insure that their customers continue to be mail-order buyers.

 Finally, there are the firms that exchange lists with both their competitors and non-competitors. Usually, only inquiries of inactive customers names are swapped. The best part of list swapping is the cost. If you normally pay $40 per thousand names for a list, you can get it for only $8 per thousand names when you swap lists. (You pay only the brokers fee, or 20% of $40.)

Functions of list brokers

The Direct Mail Association research report lists the most important services performed by list brokers.

Finds new lists—The broker is constantly seeking new lists and selecting for your consideration ones that will be of particular interest. In fact, brokers spend a great deal of their time encouraging list owners to enter the list rental field.

Acts as a clearing house for data—The broker saves you valuable time because you can go to one source for a considerable amount of information, rather than to many sources which may or may not be readily available.

Screens information—The broker carefully screens the list information provided by the list owner. Where possible he or one of his representatives personally verifies the information provided by the list owner.

Advises on testing—The broker's knowledge of the makeup of a list is often valuable in determining what will constitute a representative cross section of the list. Obviously, an error in selecting a cross section will invalidate the results of the test and possibly eliminate from your schedule a group of names that could be responsive.

Checks instructions—When you place an order with a list owner through a broker, he and his staff double check the accuracy and completeness of your instructions, thus often avoiding unnecessary misunderstandings and loss of time.

Clears offer—The broker clears for you in advance the mailing you wish to make. He supplies the list owner either with a sample of your piece or a description of it, and by getting prior approval minimizes the chance of any later disappointments.

Checks mechanics—The broker clears with the list owner the particular type of envelope, order card, or other material which is to be addressed.

Clears mailing date—When contacting the list owner, the broker checks on the mailing date which you request and asks that it be held open as a protected time for you.

Works out timing—The broker arranges either for material to be addressed or labels to be sent to you at a specified time, thus enabling you to maintain your schedule of inserting and mailing.

> *note* The broker knows the past history of many lists and usually knows the performance of which ones were previously used by other mailers.

List owner-broker relations

Get list maintenance advice—Consult with the list broker when deciding how to maintain your list so you may set it up the most practical, economical and rentable way.

Discuss rates—Discuss with your broker the price you will charge for rentals and decide on a price schedule that will bring you the greatest volume of profitable business.

Supply accurate data—Be sure the list information you furnish is accurate. If the addresses in a list were not corrected within a reasonable period of time, tell the broker.

 note If a list contains a percentage of names of people who bought on open account and failed to pay, give this information to the broker.

If you represent your list as made up entirely of buyers, be sure it does not include any inquiry or prospect names.

If you bought out a competitor and included some of their names in your customer list, be sure to state this fact.

Aside from obvious aspects of misrepresentation, you are the one who suffers when you mislead a broker.

Address on schedule—Establish a reputation for addressing on time as promised. If you accept orders and fail to fulfil them on schedule, brokers become aware of this and find they cannot conscientiously suggest your list to potential users. If, for some reason, you foresee a delay, advise the broker immediately, so he can advise the mailer.

Furnish latest counts—Keep the broker posted on current list counts, rates, changes in the sources of the names and the like. When the composition of a list changes, it may very well become more interesting to a user who previously felt that it was not suitable for his purpose. In addition, when current information is offered to a potential user through the broker, it is more likely to develop activity than is an out-dated description.

Choose brokers wisely—Consider carefully whether to make your list available to a number of list brokers or just to one broker. There are many things to be said in favor of working with several brokers. At times, there are also some good reasons for working exclusively with one broker. While the decision is yours, you should keep in mind the fact that brokers are people and each has his own particular personality, following, and sphere of influence. Therefore, as a list owner, you are well advised not to narrow the field unless your facilities for addressing are so limited that the orders one broker develop for you are more than sufficient to take up all the available addressing time.

Protect brokers—It takes a lot of time and effort on the part of a broker to interest a mailer in testing your list. Therefore, continuation runs should be scheduled through the original broker so long as he continues to render satisfactory service to his client.

> *note* The broker is a member of your sales force. Your broker can only continue to do an effective job so long as you protect him on the accounts he develops for you.

Recently there has been a trend toward list management as opposed to list brokers. A list manager takes over complete management of your list for rental purposes. Under this form of contract, the list manager is responsible for the following functions:

- He solicits his own brokerage customers directly.

- Makes all contacts with list brokers and is responsible for processing their orders.

- Should, at his own expense, advertise the list.

- Analyzes the results of each mailing and offers suggestions and advice.

- Keeps all records and is responsible for all billings.

- Provides the list owner with a detailed list of activity, along with commissions earned, etc.

For this extra service, he usually earns an additional 10%. Today, however, many list managers ask for and get more. In my opinion, they are worth the

It is not unusual for a good list manager to double or even triple your previous rental income. Naturally, some list mangers do a better job than others.

extra money. A good list manager does the utmost to promote your list. In return, the list manager earns a substantial sum of money. But, not as much as the list owner. If you decide to use a list manger instead of a broker, select the best one available. It takes some time, but it is time well spent.

I strongly suggest you subscribe to **Direct Marketing Magazine**, 224 Seventh St., Garden City, NY 11530 (http://www.idmc.org/dm.htm). This magazine will keep you abreast of the latest information available dealing with direct marketing and list selection.

How to test a list

Today the minimum number of names you are allowed to test is usually around 5,000. However, many brokers waive this rule. They do not want to lose a potentially good customer just because he or she wants to test 3,000 names instead of 5,000.

When testing a list always request Nth selection. This ensures that you are testing the effectiveness of the entire list, and not just one small segment. Nth selection simply means that the computer randomly picks a few names from the entire list. The reason you should always use Nth selection is simple, besides the obvious reason already mentioned. It stops the broker or list owner from giving you his loaded names. Many a shrewd broker or list owner will rent you only their best names when you test a list. This ensures that you get the best results possible. Later, when you return for additional names, you get the shock of your life.

Lists that are not kept up-to-date deteriorate rapidly. Many lists are totally worthless unless they are constantly cleaned.

In order for a beginner to get a trustworthy list, it might be a good idea to rent your first list from a large, reputable firm. Later, as you grow, tests can be made with lists from smaller firms. Another reason for selecting larger lists is that, should the results be rewarding, you have a larger selection of names for your future use.

Always try to rent a list consisting of buyers' names only. The more recent the better. If you cannot get a list of buyers' names only, go for a mixed list. This particular list will consist of both buyers' and inquiries' names. Once again, it is advisable to get the freshest names possible.

Always make certain that any list you decide to rent was cleaned within the last 6-12 months. Otherwise, you may be throwing your time and money away.

Who buys mailing lists

All mail-order experts agree that there is no less expensive way to increase their sales than by using the medium of direct mail. The problem all direct mail users face is where can they obtain the lists they need to continue their mailing campaigns. That is where the "mailing list dealer" comes in. By being able to supply these firms with names of authentic mail-order prospects, he or she is able to build a very successful business.

Once a firm has faith in you and the list you furnish, you can be assured that they will continue to use your service as long as you give them the same excellent service and results as in the beginning. Remember, the compiling and selling of names is a very competitive business. Yet, many aspirants, most with little or no knowledge of the business, strike it rich in this field. You must at all times offer your clients top-notch service and order-pulling lists.

How to get started

> **CAUTION** To be frank and candid, your chances of success are almost non-existent unless you have primary knowledge of mail-order selling in general. So, it would be prudent to start out in another phase of mail-order selling if you are a mail-order neophyte.

The starting supplies needed to operate a mailing list business are moderate and inexpensive. You'll definitely need a typewriter (the best one you can possibly afford). Additionally, you'll need the following supplies: letterheads and envelopes; business cards; record books; some sort of filing cabinet; sheets of perforated gummed label (available at most stationery stores); carbon paper, shipping envelopes or containers; pens and pencils and a few other supplies as you start to grow.

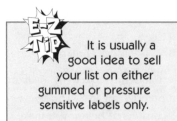

There are two ways for beginners to compile name lists: (1) On standard gummed labels, (available from your local stationery store) (2) Computer labels, from a home computer or a large main frame computer, (available from firms who specialize in this field). Since this book is primarily for beginners we first discuss the gummed labels. Later in this book, there is a section devoted to computer lists.

> **E-Z TIP** It is usually a good idea to sell your list on either gummed or pressure sensitive labels only.

Mailing lists are usually typed on sheets of perforated gummed labels ready to affix to envelopes. These standard sheets of perforated gummed labels come in 33 up sheets. Their cost is usually around $25 per thousand sheets. You can also offer the customer name lists on plain bond paper, usually there are from 35-60 names typed on a plain piece of paper. I do not generally recommend this method of name selling since it usually indicates the seller is a rank amateur.

When buying gummed, perforated labels, you should always get the ones with the carbon already inserted between each sheet of paper. In this manner, you will be able to type the name once on the original and have as many as 5 additional copies of each for sale.

Another method of reproduction of your mailing list is a copy machine. You simply insert your master copy into the machine and copy as many sheets as you need. You can do this for pressure sensitive labels as well as gummed labels. If you can afford to rent, lease or buy your own copy machine it will greatly increase your volume and also your profit potential.

> **note** As you expand, you will want to use a method that allows you to put the names in exact zip code order. This is a very important factor when selling your list of names. In the beginning, you will not have the experience or money needed to properly zip code your list.

There are many, many people using the above methods to reproduce and sell their name lists. Many are making a small fortune. But, the real big money cannot be made until you computerize your list.

Computerize your mailing list for greater profits

Probably the one question most frequently asked by mail-order list compilers is, "should I or shouldn't I computerize my list?" The answer is, "that depends." There are many factors to be considered before you make up your mind one way or the other. One thing is for sure, if computerizing your list is right for you, it will improve your profit potential in two ways. (1) By a more efficient marketing of your list (2) By increasing your income from the rental of your list.

> **note** If you plan on increasing the size and profitability of your list, computerizing your list isn't only desirable, it's virtually indispensable.

Until recently, it was not a good idea to computerize your list if it contained fewer than 15,000-20,000 names. Today, however, with the aid of small office and home computers, anyone can easily store and print out a large amount of names.

How to clean your list

> **note**

You clean your list by putting the caption "address correction requested" in the upper left hand corner of your outer envelope when you mail to your own list. Or, you can offer your customers 10 new names for every one old name they return to you. This way you do not have to send out any mailings yourself. Your customers clean the list for you.

> **note** Remember, computerized lists are like children. You have to maintain them after you bring them into the world.

List maintenance is principally a matter of adding new names, deleting "nixies" (undeliverable mail) and entering changes of address as customers move. None of these tasks are difficult, but without the proper care and dedication a good list can soon become worthless.

Where to obtain names for your list

Naturally, you can rent out your own list of customers if you have such a list. This is the way most beginners start. We previously discussed this aspect of name rentals. You can also compile other types of name lists. Examples— doctors, lawyers, drug stores, high school students, etc. Several books and directories are published that specifically deal with these types of lists. Two of the best are *Mailing List Sources,* and *Mailing List Directory*. These books are not cheap, so if you do not wish to buy them, they are available at most large public libraries. Another valuable sources for these types of lists is *Guide to American Directories for Compiling Mailing Lists.*

Another method of compiling names for a name list is to purchase the names from a mail-order dealer. The price you offer for these names is usually just a fraction of what they would cost if you paid for the advertisements. I know of one list compiler who became a very rich man using this method. He sends a form letter to mail-order dealers who advertise in the classified sections of magazines. He offers to buy their current names and all their names in the future for a fair price. After he acquires the names, he has them put on a computer listing and sells them to some of the biggest

> **note** Many small mail-order firms have no use for their names after they answer the original inquiry. They are only too glad to sell these names to the highest bidder.

mail-order firms in the country. He has done this for a long time and is the king of the opportunity-seekers name list market.

What prices to charge

Always remember to keep your list prices in line with what the other list sellers are charging. If you charge too little, most people will shy away, figuring that your list is not that good. On the other hand, if you set your price too high, most prospects will be financially unable or unwilling to spend too great a sum of money.

> **note** The price you charge for your list can vary greatly. Basically, lists, like any other commodity, have different values.

Always try to be moderate in your price structure. If you are having good results renting your list, you might try raising the price slowly and see what happens. Never jump your price too rapidly if at all possible. This tends to scare away many good prospects and old customers.

How to advertise

There are many and varied methods of reaching prospective buyers of your lists. We will discuss a few in this chapter. Remember, there are literally dozens of other ways to reach customers. We cannot and will not cover all the methods, but we attempt to cover some of the most widely used methods.

Advertise in various trade and business publications. There are magazines like *Direct Marketing Magazine* that list dozens of mailing lists in each issue. These ads are usually placed by the list broker, list manager or the list owner. This is probably the best method to use if you are going after big results. It costs a little, but it is well worth the price. You can also advertise your list in business opportunity magazines and periodicals. There are hundreds of these publications available for you to choose from. You have to test to see which one works the best for you.

> *note* Many advertisers use classified ads because they are cheap and yet reach a very large audience.

You can place classified ads in magazines. Never ask for money directly from a classified ad. These ads should be used only to solicit inquiries. When you receive the prospective buyer's inquiry, you send them all the relative information about your list. Price, names, zip code. Another very profitable method used by list sellers is to rent a list of prospective buyers from another seller. Once you attain this list, you mail out your list information to this list.

EXAMPLE: If you are selling a list containing the names of people who inquired about a book on weight-watching, you might try to rent a list of names from another dealer who is selling a book dealing with the same subject.

You would ask the other dealer to send you a list of all the people who rented his list. Since they rented his list of people interested in weight-watching, there is a good chance they would be interested in renting a similar list from you.

As stated, there are many more ways for you to reach prospective buyers. The list of inventive ways is almost endless. It is up to you to find out which method works best for you. There is no short-cut. The only way to accomplish this is by constantly testing all the methods until you hit the right one for you and for your list.

Protect your lists

If a mailer rents your list and is not specifically given permission to mail to it more than one time, and does so, then he is guilty of fraud. The Postal Service frowns on anyone who does this through the mail and the offender can be sued for damages as well. The best way to catch anyone doing this is to seed your list. Put the names and addresses of about a dozen people in the list and alert them to inform you if they receive more than one mail offer from the same person or firm. The fact that they do so does not automatically mean that you were defrauded. As you learned from the information presented, it is highly probable that the name is on more than one list. It is worth investigating though and I would investigate before filing any formal charges.

> **note** It is a fact of life that no one will want to help you if he thinks you are trying to take the food out of their family's mouths. It is no different in the list selling and compiling field.

The best way to prevent multiple mailings is to include a letter with the name list informing the renter that the list is seeded and threaten prosecution for misuse. No mailer in his right mind wants problems with Uncle Sam or his Postal Service. Such a letter will cause an unscrupulous person to have second thoughts about taking liberties with your list.

Get help from the experts

 If you need to, call some of the biggest names in the mailing list business and tell them you are interested in having your list of names managed by them. Tell them that your list contained 50,000 buyers of mail-order books. As you discuss your list, ask a few off-the-cuff questions that you need answered. Since they were interested in managing your list, they would only be too glad to answer any and all of your questions. You might say that this method is sneaky and not above board. I would say that I did what I had to do to increase my knowledge of the mailing list business.

Resources

••• Online Resources •••

◆ **American Association of Home-Based Business**

http://www.aahbb.org

◆ **American Computer Group—Mailorder.com**

http://www.mailorder.com

◆ **Antique Trader**

http://www.csmonline.com/antiquetrader

◆ **Autograph Times**

http://www.celebrityconnection.com/free.htm

◆ **Coin World**
   http://www.coinworld.com

◆ **Collectors News**
   http://collectors-news.com

◆ **Direct Marketing News**
   http://www.dmnews.com

◆ **Doll Castle News**
   http://www.dollcastlenews.com

◆ **Entrepreneur Magazine**
   http://www.entrepreneurmag.com/marketing

◆ **4 Free Net**
   http://www.4free.net

◆ **Gale Group, The**
   http://www.thomson.com/gale/default.html

◆ **Home Business Works**
   http://www.homebusinessworks.com

◆ **Listsnow.com**
   http://listsnow.com

◆ **Marketing Resource Center**

http://www.marketingsource.com

◆ **MediaFinder from Oxbridge Communications, Inc.**

http://www.mediafinder.com

◆ **National Mail Order Association, LLC**

http://www.nmoa.org

◆ **Plateau Publishing Co.: Mail Order Secrets**

http://plateaubiz.com/?linkpage

◆ **Relocatable Business Newsletter**

http://relocatable.com

◆ **ReportNet: Mail Order Business**

http://www.reportnet.net/mailorder.htm

◆ **Small Business Administration**

http://www.sba.gov

◆ **Small Business Book Mart**

http://talkbiz.com/books/banner2.html

◆ **Target Marketing**

http://www2.targetonline.com/tm/tmcover.html

◆ **U.S. Government Printing Office**

  http://www.gpo.gov

◆ **U.S. Direct Marketing Association**

  http://www.the-dma.org

◆ **Yahoo! Direct Marketing**

  http://dir.yahoo.com/Business_and_Economy/Companies/
  Marketing/Direct_Marketing/Direct_Mail

◆ **Yahoo! Mailing Lists**

  http://dir.yahoo.com/Business_and_Economy/Companies/
  Marketing/Direct_Marketing/Direct_Mail/Mailing_Lists

••• Legal Search Engines •••

◆ **All Law**
http://www.alllaw.com

◆ **American Law Sources On Line**
http://www.lawsource.com/also/searchfm.htm

◆ **Catalaw**
http://www.catalaw.com

◆ **FindLaw**
http://www.findlaw.com

◆ **InternetOracle**
http://www.internetoracle.com/legal.htm

◆ **LawAid**
http://www.lawaid.com/search.html

◆ **LawCrawler**
http://www.lawcrawler.com

◆ **LawEngine, The**
http://www.fastsearch.com/law

◆ **LawRunner**
http://www.lawrunner.com

◆ 'Lectric Law Library™
   http://www.lectlaw.com

◆ Legal Search Engines
   http://www.dreamscape.com/frankvad/search.legal.html

◆ LEXIS/NEXIS Communications Center
   http://www.lexis-nexis.com/lncc/general/search.html

◆ Meta-Index for U.S. Legal Research
   http://gsulaw.gsu.edu/metaindex

◆ Seamless Website, The
   http://seamless.com

◆ USALaw
   http://www.usalaw.com/linksrch.cfm

◆ WestLaw
   http://westdoc.com (Registered users only. Fee paid service.)

••• Mail-Order Resources •••

◆ A.A. Archbald, P.O. Box 57985, Los Angeles, CA 90057—offers many books of printed cuts, type fonts, borders, etc., for offset printing paste-ups.

◆ Ace Toy. 1545a Coney Island Avenue, Brooklyn, New York 11230 (718) 434-7233. Wholesale toys. Ask for catalog.

◆ Addressing Machine & Equipment Co., 383 Lafayette, New York, NY 10003—offers rebuilt offset printing presses at lowest prices. Write.

◆ "African-Asian Markets," P.O. Box 325, Bombay 1, India—write for their Trade Journal. Write on your letterhead.

◆ African Woodcarvings, Inc., 260 5th Ave., New York, NY 10011—offers low priced African woodcarvings. Write.

◆ Amity Hallmark, Ltd., P.O. Box 1148, Linden Hill Sta., Flushing, NY 11354—offers 1,000 8 1/2 x 11 circulars printed and postpaid for only $4.95. Write.

◆ Arco Publishing Co., 480 Lexington Ave, New York, NY 10017—offers self-help books at lowest wholesale cost. Write.

◆ Asian Imports, 6902 20th Avenue, Hyattsville, MD 20783—offers free drop-ship catalog of Asian products.

◆ Atlas Associates, 5 Matter Strasse, 85 Nuernberg/Eiback, Germany—drop-ships imitation 400-day clock. Write.

◆ Baby Supply Catalog for 25¢ from Volz Enterprises, 602 Ferris St., Ypsilanti, MI 48197. Dealership available. Firm will drop-ship.

◆ Brewster Sales, 808 Washington, St. Louis, MO 63101—send for 100 2-color name and address labels. Small fee.

◆ Business Envelope Manufacturers, Inc., Pearl River, NY 10965—will print #10 envelopes for as low as $3.60 per 1,000 and Return Address envelopes for as low as $2.60 per 1,000. Printed 2-color letterheads for $8.80 per 1,000. Write for free list.

◆ Champion Printing Co., Box 148, Ross, OH 45061—will drop-ship printing orders to your customers.

- Coin World, P.O. Box 150, Sidney, OH 45365—write for copy of "Basic Knowledge for the Coin Collector."

- Collectors News, Box 156, Grundy Center, IA 50638—write for a free copy of their publication.

- Copen Press, 100 Berriman St., Brooklyn, NY 11208—will print 8-page catalogs or booklets for as low as 1.5 cents each. Write for price list.

- Court Knitwear, Ltd., Court Devenish, Athione, Ireland—write for information and prices on their pure-wool hand-knitted sweaters. Firm will drop-ship.

- Cuckoo Clock Mfg. Co., Inc., 40 W. 25th St., New York, NY 10001—write for catalog and prices of cuckoo, wall, alarm and mantle clocks.

- Davis Book Wholesales, Inc. 115 E. 23rd St., New York, NY 10010—offers surplus and closeout books at wholesale prices. Write.

- East Asia Publishing Co., 298, 3-chrome, Harajuku, Shibuya-ku, Tokyo, Japan.—Get copy of "Oriental America"

- Earl P.L. Appelbaum, Inc., 1420 Walnut, Philadelphia, PA 19102—write for periodical catalogs of Stamp Mail-Bid auctions.

- Federal, 6652 N. Western, Chicago, IL 60645—offers 1-dozen vinyl records for only $18.00. Ask for free catalog.

- Fritz S. Hogheimer, Inc., 29 E. 22nd St., New York, NY 10010—Get free 120-page catalog of 120,000 mailing lists

- George W. Halings, P.O. Box 265, Carlsbad, CA 92008—Get free report on "Coin Investing."

- Guild Mail Order House, 103 E. Broadway, New York, NY 10002— offers used factory-cleaned sport coats and suits for $5.75 and $9.95. Free catalog.

- Gutmann Cutlery Co., Inc., 3956 Broadway, New York, NY 10006— offers imported knives, fishing and hunting equipment at importer prices.

- Hams Publications, 224 Market St., Newark, NJ 07102. Get free 42-page catalog of mailing lists.

◆ Handleather Co., Box 282, Nestor, CA 92053—Get catalog of Mexican leather purses, wallets and vests.

◆ Harlow Geographics, Box 23, Kingston, MA 02360—offers old National Geographics for as low as 50 cents each. Write for price lists.

◆ Hi-Test Premier Products, Inc., 361 Broadway, New York, NY 10006—offers quality low cost imported tools. Write.

◆ H.L. Randall, 2160 Nokomis, St. Paul, MN 55119—send requested fee for 16-page buying list of old books.

◆ Harpeng Liang, P.O. Box 1765, Bangkok, Thailand—send requested fee for information on products they will drop-ship.

◆ Home Business Digest, P.O. Box 839, Long Beach, NY 11561—sample catalog and instructions on how to make $100 weekly mailing catalogs.

◆ Hong Kong Enterprise, Ocean Terminal, 2nd Deck, Lantoo Gallery, Kowloon, Hong Kong—write for copy of their Trade Journal. Write on your letterhead.

◆ Hong Kong Trade Development Council, Ocean Terminal, Kowloon, Hong Kong—will give free information on firms and products from Hong Kong.

◆ Irish Export Board, Lansdowne House, Ballsbridge, Dublin 4, Ireland—will give information on firms and products of Ireland.

◆ Imperial Merchandise Co., 22 W. 23rd St., New York, NY 10010—write for catalog of imported products.

◆ Itraco Watch Co., Zurich I, Switzerland—will drop-ship low-cost and premium watches to your customer.

◆ Jacobi Industries, 1715 E. Mercer, Seattle, WA 98102—offers free wholesale catalog of jewelry, watches and gifts.

◆ Jakla Gem, Box 3066, Seminole, FL 33542—offers diamond-like rings as low as $5.00 each.

◆ Japan Trade Monthly, Dentsu Bldg., Tokyo, Japan. Get copy of "Japan Trade Monthly."

◆ Jeros Tackle Co., Inc., 111 16th St., Brooklyn, NY—offers all kinds of fishing tackle at importers prices. Write.

◆ Lakeside Imports Co., 6800 N. Campbell, Chicago, IL 60645—offers free wholesale catalog of over 100 fast sellers.

◆ Mailers Equipment Co., Inc., 40 W. 15th St., New York, NY 10011—offers factory rebuilt address machines and mailing equipment. Write on letterhead.

◆ Mashburn's, P.O. Box 118-W, Enka, NC 28728—will pay up to $1.00 each for cards and letters postmarked before 1915. Send stamp for list. Buys old pocket knives, baseball cards. Write giving name, tracing and full description of knives. Stamped envelope will get best offer. Send $1.00 for copy of "Foreign Publications Directory."

◆ Mashburn Coins, Enka, NC 28728—will buy old coins at highest dealer prices for buying. List dates, mint and condition of your coins. Enclose stamp for highest offer by return mail.

◆ Metro, 60 South St., Boston, MA 02111 offers free closeout lists.

◆ Mexican Importing Co., North Pacific, Albany, OR 97321—offers Mexican feather-bird pictures at jobber prices. Send 25¢ for sample pictures and prices.

◆ Multicraft, P.O. Box 4119, Rotterdam, Netherlands—offers free drop-ship catalog.

◆ Merrill & Co., 7 Bennett St., Battle Creek, MI 49017—offers 1,000 quality red border shipping labels for $6.50. Write.

◆ Mid-America Book Co., Main Street, Leon, IA 50144—offers free catalog of hundreds of books on antiques.

◆ Music Enterprises, P.O. Box 55088, Sherman Oaks, CA 91413—offers factory-fresh 8-track tapes for as low as 80¢ each, postpaid. Write.

◆ Music, P.O. Box 3305, Beverly Hills, CA 90213—offers new 45 RPM records for 4¢ each and LP records for 40¢ each. Write.

- Nectar Label Co., 34 Hubert St., New York, NY 10013—offers low cost high quality shipping labels. Write for price list.

- Old Colonial Anderson Mills, Dalton, GA 30720—offers free catalog of irregular bedspreads for as low as $1.60 each. Write.

- Otto Gruenhut Co., 377 Broadway, New York, NY 10013—offers pens and pencils at lowest wholesale prices.

- Penny Label Co., 9-15 Murray St., New York, NY 10007—offers lowest prices on gummed perforated addressing labels and other labels.

- Publishers Exchange, P.O. Box 1355, Sioux Falls, SD 57101. Get free Newsletter, "Selling Books By Mail."

- Quality Office Equipment Corp., 166 W. 23rd St., New York, NY 10011— Get electric IBM typewriters for as low as $89.50 and others at $19.95.

- Rudi Klenzier, 7745 Schonach, Germany—offers catalog of hand carved souvenirs and clocks.

- Rugby Press, 3321 Ave. N, Brooklyn, NY 11234—offers personalized memo pads (1,000 sheets).

- Rutward Publications, Box 735-M, Norwalk, CT 06852—for copy of "Profits in Mail Order."

- Sheldon Cord Products, 3320 W. Lawrence Ave., Chicago, IL 60625—offers a catalog of products below wholesale. Send $1.00 for catalog.

- Small Business Administration, Washington, DC 20416—Get directory of 92 Mailing List Houses.

- South Bay Enterprises, 65 "I" St. Chula Vista, CA 92010—offers free wholesale catalog of Mexican hand-tooled purses.

- Southern Watches, 5 South Wabash, Chicago, IL 60603—offers free list of pocket and wrist watches starting at $3.00 each. Write.

- Stephens Products Co., 2160 Broadway, New York, NY 10023—write for free wholesale catalog of costume and personalized jewelry.

- Success International, Box 2447, Livonia, MI 48151. Get copy of "How to Become Rich."

- Sumberg Enterprises, Dept. "Coins," 331 Eastern Ave., Maiden, MA 02148 offers wholesale coin supplies and books. Write.

- T. Mason Sales Co., 957 N. Lewis Ave., Waukegan, IL 60085 offers check writers and money-making details for only $5.00 each for first sample.

- Taiwan Handicraft Promotion Center, Schung Shan Rd., S., Taipei, Taiwan, Formosa—write for free copy of "China Handicraft Industry" monthly.

- Trapkus Art Studio, 5120 11th Ave., Moline, IL 61265—low cost producer of art work for your product or service.

- Turnbaugh Services, Mechanicsburg, PA 17055. Get free catalog of new and used printing machinery, supplies and equipment.

- Unity Buying Service, Inc., Mt. Vernon, NY 10551—information on buying name brands at factory prices, plus 5% handling charge.

- U.S. Government Printing Office, Washington, DC—offers a free list of directories and books they publish.

- U.S. Small Business Administration, Washington, DC 20416. Get free book "Selling by Mail Order"

- U.S. Chamber of Commerce in Germany, Taunusantage 21, Frankfurt A.M., West Germany. Write for free copy of "Commerce in Germany."

- Warshawsky & Co., 1900-24 S. State St., Chicago, IL 60616 for their wholesale automotive parts and accessories catalog.

- Wm. Stroh, Inc., 568-570 54th St., West New York, NJ 07083 will pay up to $25.00 per 1,000 for your inquiry letters.

- World Trade Inquiries, Hillyard, WA 99207 for copy of Japan-Hong Kong Directory.

••• Free Commission Circulars •••

This list was current at time of publication. However, suppliers sometimes change their policy. Most offer free circulars, you pay only the postage costs.

A & M Sales Co., 3241 Hayne Ave., Chicago, IL 60618;

Ace Products, Box 333, Shreveport, LA 71103;

Atlanta Press, 1600 Hawthorne Dr., Chesapeake, VA 23325;

Cavazos Advertising, 1952 S. King Rd., San Jose, CA 95122;

A & H Sales Co., Box 579, Cambridge, MD 21613;

Astro Sales Co., Box 8901, Houston, TX 77009;

Badburd Sales Co., 2559 Josephine St., Lynwood, CA 90262;

Burco Sales Co., 39 Wyoming Ave., Ardmore, PA 19003;

Barbies Shop, 347 Malden, Newport News, VA 22202;

Chicago Mail Mart, 8408 Buffalo Ave, Chicago, IL 60617,

Cooleys Enterprises, Box 161, Signal Mtn., TN 37337;

Danzig Enterprises, Box 142, Kensington Sta., Brooklyn, NY 11218;

Dawde Enterprises, 9254 Manning Ave., Stillwater, MN 55082;

Gradco Publications, Box 23436, Milwaukee, WI 53223;

Jack Clamp, Box 144, Hastings-on-Hudson, NY 10706;

Lew Card, Box 392, Vrea, CA 92621;

Midwest Mail Sales, Box 44RS, Shawano, WI 54166,

Martels, Box 607, Median, ND 58134;

Progressive Publications, Box 3770, Clear Lake Highlands, CA 95422;

Ray Holder, Box 91, O'Keen, AR 72449;

Royal Sales Co., Box 17515, El Paso, TX 79914;

Sandcos Publications, Box 3414, 9th St., Ceres, CA 95307;

Success Publishers, Box 68, Webb City, MO 64870.

••• Mail-Order Publications •••

Here is a list of the four best publications to put your advertisements in:

Mail Order Opportunity Weekly

Mail Order Bulletin

Popular Advertiser

Ben Franklin's Almanac.

For a sample issue of each, send two First Class Stamps to:

Wayne's Printing, Rt. 2, Myrtle, MS 38650

Plus, here is a list of other publishers to contact:

Berwick's, 15 E. Devane St., Pensacola FL 32514

GD Services, PO Box 80, Foyil, OK 74031

Ida L. Edmonds, Rt 1 Box 373, Bernie, MO 63823

Odds & Ends, PO Box 10797, Chicago, IL 60610

Profit Tools, 3824 Elm Lane, Oshkosh, WI 54901

Wolf Enterprises, 111 Carmichael Ct., Cary, NC 27512

Youngers, PO Box 37, Princeton, IA 52768

••• Free Mailing Lists •••

These sources provide you with a free mailing list. Usually in list form, so that you have to re-type each names on your mailing piece. They obtain these names in many different ways. They are usually opportunity seekers, buyers, or people who paid to be listed. Each source requires a self-addressed envelope, and two first-class postage stamps. Each list usually contains about 200 or more names:

Beavers, Box 509, McCaysville, GA 30555

Cavazos Advertising, 1952 S. King Road, San Jose, CA 95122;

C. Walker, 6250 Babcock Ave., N. Hollywood, CA 91606;

Erma Majors Co., 3134 N. Achilles, Milwaukee, WI 53212;

French Express, 8403 Anthony Wayne Ave., Cincinnati, OH 45216

Heath Books, 33 Irving Ave., Providence, RI 02906;

Jackson Publications, Box 419-FML, West Haven, CT 06516

Jay David Co., Box 5, McFarlon, NC 28102.

Lew Card, Box 392, Brea, CA 92621;

Northside Studios, Box 320, Silver Springs, MD 20907

Prichards, 805 NW Avenue "J", Seminole, TX 79360;

Square Deal Co., Box 272, Gordonsville, VA 22942;

TJ Enterprises, Box 4960, Washington, DC 20008;

Wellmans, Box 571, Chase City, VA 23924

Willards Salles Co., PO Box 1036, Palm Springs, CA 92262

••• Mail-Order Publishers •••

James Lepore
363 Miller Ave.
Freeport, NY 11520

Yesterday's Magazette
PO Box 15126
Sarasota, FL 34277

North American Messenger
Box 335
Stoughton, MA 02072

Larry Chiappone
Box 1152
W. Babylon, NY 11704

Edwards Publishing Co.
Box 913
Bristol, VA 24203

Bob Tinsdale
PO Box 517
Stillwater, NY 12170

L R Guill/Lile's Advertiser
RR 3 Box 645
Rustburg, VA 24588

USA Business Monthly
Box 42 Whiton Road
Antrim, NH 03440

Crafts and Collections
PO Box 291
Portland, CT 06480-0291

Paul Metcalf
RR 3 Centerville Road
Richland, NY 13144-9801

Niagara Promotions
PO Box 988
Lewiston, NY 14092

Randy Wolf
111 Carmichael Ct.
Cary, NC 27511

Network Co-op Ad Sheet
PO Box 90423
Rochester, NY 14609

Giannino/Fortuna Int'l
20 Ginkgo Ct.
Upper Saddle River, NJ 07458

Circle of Friends
371 Valley View Road
Claysville, PA 15323-9418

Keystone State Mailer
57 Amm Street
Bradford, PA 16701

Bad Guys Newsletter
Box 7600
Newark, DE 19711

Jerry Stokes
PO Box 416
Taylors, SC 29687

Valerie Vals
1883 Billingsly Terrace
Bronx, NY 10453

Advantage Advertiser
3025 Belvedere Cr.
Decatur, GA 30035

American Book Collector
Box 867
Ossining, NY 10562-0867

Todd Publications
18 Greenbush Road
W. Nyack, NY 10094-2008

Tom's Hot Sheet
RR 2 Box 295
Quinton, VA 23141

WK Snapp/TNT Publications
Box 10394
Jacksonville, FL 32247

S Yager/Infinity Advertiser
8435 Lander Street
Jamaica, NY 11435

Clover Distributing Co.
3908 Providence Road
Chesapeake, VA 23325

The Indo Society
31 Olive Road
Ocala, FL 32678

Global Bulletin
1520 Ave. G Ensley
Birmingham, AL 35218

The National Hobby News
Box 612
New Philadelphia, OH 44663

Worldwide Advertiser
PO Box 538
Reform, AL 35481

Lelli Printing/Advertising
2650 CR. 175
Loudonville, OH 44842

N M Burkhalter
5 Margaret Ave.
Chickasaw, AL 36611

G. Bayshore
5260 N. Walnut Street
Covington, OH 45318

Office At Home Advertiser
RR 4 Box 1134-A
Little Torch Key, FL 33042

Beeler's Advertiser
RR 3 Mount Olive Road
Knoxville, TN 37920

Prosperity Concept
4335 Hunt Cliff Tr.
Memphis, TN 38187

Mail Order Messenger
PO Box 17131
Memphis, TN 38187

Nicky's Shopper
4450 NW 22nd Street
Lauderhill, FL 33313

Anchor Advertiser
PO Box 2181
Kettering, OH 45429

MO Opportunity Weekly
RR 2
Myrtle, MS 38650

Hobby News/Homeworkers
RR 2 Box 42
McCall Creek, MS 39647

Optimax
Box 88256
Indianapolis, IN 46208

National M
PO Box 5
Sarasota, FL 34230

United Mail Order Systems
PO Box 579
Big Pine Key, FL 33043

Gene Orefice
1221 NW 45th Street
Pompano Beach, FL 33064

M O Success Newsletter
PO Box 14705
Dayton, OH 45414

National Traders Journal
PO Box 560
Troy, TN 38260

Broadway Publishers
7546 Palm Road
West Palm Beach, FL 33406

Million Dollar Advertiser
309 S. Third Street
Ironton, OH 45638

Steven D. Brown
230 E. Southern Heights
Louisville, KY 40209

The Gator Trader
130-R Patterson Road N
Ft. Myers, FL 33903

Bluegrass Advertiser
RR 1 Box 869-H
Pikeville, KY 41501

The Mail Box %
Heflin Printing Center
2846 Lagrange Street
Toledo, OH 43608-2355

Sutton's Handy Shopper
11565 Ridgewood Circle N
Seminole, FL 34642

Stilson and Stilson
PO Box 1075
Tarpon Springs, FL 34688

Opportunity Weekly Magazine
1313 Sneak Road
Foristell, MO 63348

Artcraft Press
PO Box 225
Mankato, MN 56001-0225

Opportunity Express
PO Box 953
Baldwin, MI 49304

Elmer Van Houten
RR 2 Box 79
Humboldt, KS 66748

Hotsheet Advertiser
PO Box 607
Medina, ND 58467-0607

Performance Plus
1022 N. Gennesee Road
Burton, MI 46509

John W. Glaefke
2619 Hearthstone
Parma, OH 44134

Income & Business Opp. Magazine
PO Box 398
Side Lake, MN 55718-0398

Paul E. Skeens
PO Box 311
Jackson, MI 49204

Theresa J. White
6558 W. 51st Street
Mission, KS 66202

Virginia Pritchard
904 N. French Ave.
Sioux Falls, SD 57103

G. L. Williams
1801 S. Cardinal Lane
New Berlin, WI 53151

Bus/Career Opportunities
3015 Woodsdale Blvd.
Lincoln, NE 68502-5053

Endless Advertiser
PO Box 556
Middleton, WI 53562-0556

Profit$ Magazine
PO Box 4785
Lincoln, NE 68504

Money Maker's Monthly
Box 7116
Villa Park, IL 60181

Photo Source International
Pine Lake Farm
Oscfola, WI 54020

Partners In Publishing
Box 50347
Tulsa, OK 74150

R G Bergmann
PO Box 1
Saxon, WI 54557-0001

Business Opportunity News
PO Box 18571
Dallas, TX 75218

Delta Publishing Co.
PO Box 46
Cooper, TX 75432

Linda Shields
Box 690
Hallsville, TX 75650

Leap Ahead Advertiser
1019 Utah Avenue
Libby, MT 59923

Joan Anderson
Box S13
Beaver Dam, WI 53916

Bill Drinkard
4733 SE 17th
Del City, OK 73115

Bob Newly/Profitable Opp.
3 Golf Center #311
Hoffman Estates. IL 60195

Dwight Early
405 N Wabash Ave. #1514
Chicago, IL 60611

Mail Marketing News Advertiser
4550 Malden
Chicago, IL 60640

Midwest/Ideas Unlimited
520 Jefferson Street
Oshkosh, WI 54901

Looney/Family Travel Log
Box 406
K E Wanee, IL 61443

National Handicrafter Opp.
1123 Edmund
St. Paul, MN 55104

Up Your Income Advertiser
Box 545
Nocona, TX 76255

Universal New Products Mag.
1669 S. Voss Road #V
Houston, TX 77057

Interstate Enterprises
Box 19689
Houston, TX 77224

Mail Dealer Service
Box 2693
Covina, CA 91722

M O Times/Inner Circle
1609 Paloma Street
Barstow, CA 92311

Dustbooks
PO Box 100
Paradise, CA 95967

N. Amer. Book Dealers Exchg
PO Box 606
Cottage Grove, OR 97424

Cha Services
2830 La Pine Avenue
Central Point, OR 97502

T A Supply Co/Mini-Mailer
Box 42386
Las Vegas, NV 89104

Walter Homan
Box 6644
St. Paul, MN 55106

Randol's Advertiser
8425 Pennsylvania Ave.
St. Louis, MO 63111

Texmo Advertiser
806 W. Stamper
Beesville, TX 78102

Adventure of Mr. M O
1460 Boulder Ave.
Crescent City, CA 95531

BC Studio Publications
PO Box 5908
Huntington Beach, CA 92615

George Norr
PO Box 70268
Salt Lake City, UT 84170

Arizona Advertiser
3290 Tower Road
Prescott Valley, AZ 86314

G Bridgeman/G & B Records
Box 150
Terra Bella, CA 93270

Linda's Millionaire
Box 104
Vista Grande, CA 94016

J. Buchanan/Towers Club
PO Box 2038
Vancouver, WA 98668

Fun Mates Press-Dept. GNFE
PO Box 426466
San Francisco, CA 94142

The American Mailer
Box 20315
Reno, NV 89515

The Simmon's Company
PO Box 880761
San Francisco, CA 94188-0761

D Hermon/It's In The Mail
Box 1117 - Sqaumish
B.C., Canada V0N 3GO

Los Angeles Advertiser
3119 Isabel Drive
Los Angeles, CA 90065

Gold Service
PO Box 508
Duarte, CA 91010

Singles Critique
PO Box 5062
Sherman Oaks, CA 91413-5062

Flea Market Directory
PO Box 640
Keyes, CA 95328-0640

Jim Little
PO Box 2311
Turlock, CA 95381-2311

Appendix

100 words that have sales appeal

Add sale punch to describe your merchandise or sales offer—use one of the following words. It may be helpful used alone or with other words. They have been selected from successful ads for convenience in preparing your copy.

Absolutely	Fascinating	Miracle	Sensational
Amazing	Fortune	Noted	Simplified
Approved	Full	Odd	Sizable
Attractive	Genuine	Outstanding	Special
Authentic	Gift	Personalized	Startling
Bargain	Gigantic	Popular	Strange
Beautiful	Greatest	Powerful	Strong
Better	Guaranteed	Practical	Sturdy
Big	Helpful	Professional	Successful
Colorful	Highest	Profitable	Superior
Colossal	Huge	Profusely.	Surprise
Complete	Immediately	Proven	Terrific
Confidential	Improved	Quality	Tested
Crammed	Informative	Quickly	Tremendous
Delivered	Instructive	Rare	Unconditional
Direct	Interesting	Reduced	Unique
Discount	Largest	Refundable	Unlimited
Easily	Latest	Remarkable	Unparalleled
Endorsed	Lavishly	Reliable	Unsurpassed
Enormous	Liberal	Revealing	Unusual
Excellent	Lifetime	Revolutionary	Useful
Exciting	Limited	Scarce	Valuable
Exclusive	Lowest	Secrets	Wealth
Expert	Magic	Security	Weird
Famous	Mammoth	Selected	Wonderful

70 phrases stimulating action

Close your ad with an action-getting phrase. Give the reader something to write or do. Here are 70 suggestions for ways to get action. Study them. They will help you prepare your copy for better results.

Act now!
Send your name
All sent free to introduce
Amazing literature . . . Free
Ask for free folder
Bargain lists sent free
Be first to qualify
Booklet free!
Catalog included free
Complete details free
Current list free
Dealers write for prices
Description sent free
Details free!
Dime brings details
Everything supplied!
Exciting details free
Extra for promptness
First lesson, 25 cents
Folder free!
For literature, write:
Free booklet explains
Free plans tell how
Free selling kit
Free wholesale plan
Free with approvals
Full particulars free
Get facts that help
Get started today!
Get your copy now!
Get yours wholesale
Gifts with purchases
Illustrated lists free
nteresting details free
Investigate today
It's Free! . . . Act Now!.

Literature free.
Mail material to:
Money making facts free
No obligation! Write!
Offer limited!
Send today
Only 10 cents to introduce
Order direct from:
Order Now!
Don't Delay!
Particulars free
Postcard brings details
Request free literature
Revealing booklet free
Rush name for details
Sales kit furnished
Sample details free
Samples sent on trial
See before you buy
Send for free details
Send for it today
Send no money
Send post card today
Send 15 cents for mailing
Send toda
Send your want lists
Stamp brings details
Stamped envelope brings
Test lesson free
Unique sample offer
Valuable details free
Write for free booklet free
Write us first!
Yours for the asking
33 cent stamp for details
$1 for complete 32-page catalog free

The 100 most threatening spelling words in the order of their "threat" to you

occasion	judgment	apparent	beginning
recommend	quantity	calendar	especially
occurred	similar	professor	volume
principal	undoubtedly	strictly	committee
equipped	height	principle	confident
accommodate	immediately	already	difference
disappoint	stationery	coming	endeavor
possession	foreign	its	explanation
privilege	fourth	oblige	except
proceed	government	opportunity	sincerely
inconvenience	omitted	original	experience
accept	weather	paid	benefited
business	personnel	probably	conscientious
necessary	existence	referring	eligible
personal	analysis	referred	acquaintance
receive	across	there	controversy
reference	appearance	too	exceed
separate	loose	writing	laboratory
their	pamphlet	among	omission
whether	practical	arrangement	procedure
questionnaire	preferred	practically	acknowledgment
criticism	unnecessary	convenient	Wednesday
description	affect	canceled	guarantee
effect	attendance	really	February
extension	incidentally	using	schedule

The Key is to combine your words: example: "the magic mammouth miracle"; "The Three "M" Program"... This has already caught the attention and interest of your prospect! Now... for example say: The Money Making Facts are FREE! Merely Enclose your LSASE or $$ or Whatever! Fill in with a few details and you have a tremendous $$ Pulling Ad. Use your own Ideas, but build them around these words and phrases! but remember, your follow-up material, must be just as interesting to get the orders. NOW: A little test... did you catch the misspelling of Mammoth (Mammouth)... well it's correct either way - the "ou" is used by the British!

How to save on attorney fees

How to save on attorney fees

Millions of Americans know they need legal protection, whether it's to get agreements in writing, protect themselves from lawsuits, or document business transactions. But too often these basic but important legal matters are neglected because of something else millions of Americans know: legal services are expensive.

They don't have to be. In response to the demand for affordable legal protection and services, there are now specialized clinics that process simple documents. Paralegals help people prepare legal claims on a freelance basis. People find they can handle their own legal affairs with do-it-yourself legal guides and kits. Indeed, this book is a part of this growing trend.

When are these alternatives to a lawyer appropriate? If you hire an attorney, how can you make sure you're getting good advice for a reasonable fee? Most importantly, do you know how to lower your legal expenses?

When there is no alternative

Make no mistake: serious legal matters require a lawyer. The tips in this book can help you reduce your legal fees, but there is no alternative to good professional legal services in certain circumstances:

- when you are charged with a felony, you are a repeat offender, or jail is possible

- when a substantial amount of money or property is at stake in a lawsuit

- when you are a party in an adversarial divorce or custody case

- when you are an alien facing deportation

- when you are the plaintiff in a personal injury suit that involves large sums of money

- when you're involved in very important transactions

Are you sure you want to take it to court?

Consider the following questions before you pursue legal action:

What are your financial resources?

Money buys experienced attorneys, and experience wins over first-year lawyers and public defenders. Even with a strong case, you may save money by not going to court. Yes, people win millions in court. But for every big winner there are ten plaintiffs who either lose or win so little that litigation wasn't worth their effort.

Do you have the time and energy for a trial?

Courts are overbooked, and by the time your case is heard your initial zeal may have grown cold. If you can, make a reasonable settlement out of court. On personal matters, like a divorce or custody case, consider the emotional toll on all parties. Any legal case will affect you in some way. You will need time away from work. A newsworthy case may bring press coverage. Your loved ones, too, may face publicity. There is usually good reason to settle most cases quickly, quietly, and economically.

How can you settle disputes without litigation?

Consider *mediation*. In mediation, each party pays half the mediator's fee and, together, they attempt to work out a compromise informally. *Binding arbitration* is another alternative. For a small fee, a trained specialist serves as judge, hears both sides, and hands down a ruling that both parties have agreed to accept.

So you need an attorney

Having done your best to avoid litigation, if you still find yourself headed for court, you will need an attorney. To get the right attorney at a reasonable cost, be guided by these four questions:

What type of case is it?

You don't seek a foot doctor for a toothache. Find an attorney experienced in your type of legal problem. If you can get recommendations from clients who have recently won similar cases, do so.

Where will the trial be held?

You want a lawyer familiar with that court system and one who knows the court personnel and the local protocol—which can vary from one locality to another.

Should you hire a large or small firm?

Hiring a senior partner at a large and prestigious law firm sounds reassuring, but chances are the actual work will be handled by associates—at high rates. Small firms may give your case more attention but, with fewer resources, take longer to get the work done.

What can you afford?

Hire an attorney you can afford, of course, but know what a fee quote includes. High fees may reflect a firm's luxurious offices, high-paid staff and unmonitored expenses, while low estimates may mean "unexpected" costs later. Ask for a written estimate of all costs and anticipated expenses.

How to find a good lawyer

Whether you need an attorney quickly or you're simply open to future possibilities, here are seven nontraditional methods for finding your lawyer:

1) **Word of mouth**: Successful lawyers develop reputations. Your friends, business associates and other professionals are potential referral sources. But beware of hiring a friend. Keep the client-attorney relationship strictly business.

2) **Directories**: The Yellow Pages and the Martin-Hubbell Lawyer Directory (in your local library) can help you locate a lawyer with the right education, background and expertise for your case.

3) **Databases**: A paralegal should be able to run a quick computer search of local attorneys for you using the Westlaw or Lexis database.

4) **State bar associations**: Bar associations are listed in phone books. Along with lawyer referrals, your bar association can direct you to low-cost legal clinics or specialists in your area.

5) **Law schools**: Did you know that a legal clinic run by a law school gives law students hands-on experience? This may fit your legal needs. A third-year law student loaded with enthusiasm and a little experience might fill the bill quite inexpensively—or even for free.

6) **Advertisements**: Ads are a lawyer's business card. If a "TV attorney" seems to have a good track record with your kind of case, why not call? Just don't be swayed by the glamour of a high-profile attorney.

7) **Your own ad**: A small ad describing the qualifications and legal expertise you're seeking, placed in a local bar association journal, may get you just the lead you need.

How to hire and work with your attorney

No matter how you hear about an attorney, you must interview him or her in person. Call the office during business hours and ask to speak to the attorney directly. Then explain your case briefly and mention how you obtained the attorney's name. If the attorney sounds interested and knowledgeable, arrange for a visit.

The ten-point visit

1) Note the address. This is a good indication of the rates to expect.

2) Note the condition of the offices. File-laden desks and poorly maintained work space may indicate a poorly run firm.

3) Look for up-to-date computer equipment and an adequate complement of support personnel.

4) Note the appearance of the attorney. How will he or she impress a judge or jury?

5) Is the attorney attentive? Does the attorney take notes, ask questions, follow up on points you've mentioned?

6)   Ask what schools he or she has graduated from, and feel free to check credentials with the state bar association.

7)   Does the attorney have a good track record with your type of case?

8)   Does he or she explain legal terms to you in plain English?

9)   Are the firm's costs reasonable?

10) Will the attorney provide references?

Hiring the attorney

Having chosen your attorney, make sure all the terms are agreeable. Send letters to any other attorneys you have interviewed, thanking them for their time and interest in your case and explaining that you have retained another attorney's services.

Request a letter from your new attorney outlining your retainer agreement. The letter should list all fees you will be responsible for as well as the billing arrangement. Did you arrange to pay in installments? This should be noted in your retainer agreement.

Controlling legal costs

Legal fees and expenses can get out of control easily, but the client who is willing to put in the effort can keep legal costs manageable. Work out a budget with your attorney. Create a timeline for your case. Estimate the costs involved in each step.

Legal fees can be straightforward. Some lawyers charge a fixed rate for a specific project. Others charge contingency fees (they collect a percentage of your recovery, usually 35-50 percent if you win and nothing if you lose). But most attorneys prefer to bill by the hour. Expenses can run the gamut, with one hourly charge for taking depositions and another for making copies.

Have your attorney give you a list of charges for services rendered and an itemized monthly bill. The bill should explain the service performed, who performed the work, when the service was provided, how long it took, and how the service benefits your case.

Ample opportunity abounds in legal billing for dishonesty and greed. There is also plenty of opportunity for knowledgeable clients to cut their bills significantly if they know what to look for. Asking the right questions and setting limits on fees is smart and can save you a bundle. Don't be afraid to question legal bills. It's your case and your money!

When the bill arrives

- **Retainer fees**: You should already have a written retainer agreement. Ideally, the retainer fee applies toward case costs, and your agreement puts that in writing. Protect yourself by escrowing the retainer fee until the case has been handled to your satisfaction.

- **Office visit charges**: Track your case and all documents, correspondence, and bills. Diary all dates, deadlines and questions you want to ask your attorney during your next office visit. This keeps expensive office visits focused and productive, with more accomplished in less time. If your attorney charges less for phone consultations than office visits, reserve visits for those tasks that must be done in person.

- **Phone bills**: This is where itemized bills are essential. Who made the call, who was spoken to, what was discussed, when was the call made, and how long did it last? Question any charges that seem unnecessary or excessive (over 60 minutes).

- **Administrative costs**: Your case may involve hundreds, if not thousands, of documents: motions, affidavits, depositions, interrogatories, bills, memoranda, and letters. Are they all necessary? Understand your attorney's case strategy before paying for an endless stream of costly documents.

- **Associate and paralegal fees**: Note in your retainer agreement which staff people will have access to your file. Then you'll have an informed and efficient staff working on your case, and you'll recognize their names on your bill. Of course, your attorney should handle the important part of your case, but less costly paralegals or associates may handle routine matters more economically. Note: Some firms expect their associates to meet a quota of billable hours, although the time spent is not always warranted. Review your bill. Does the time spent make sense for the document in question? Are several staff involved in matters that should be handled by one person? Don't be afraid to ask questions. And withhold payment until you have satisfactory answers.

- **Court stenographer fees**: Depositions and court hearings require costly transcripts and stenographers. This means added expenses. Keep an eye on these costs.

- **Copying charges**: Your retainer fee should limit the number of copies made of your complete file. This is in your legal interest, because multiple files mean multiple chances others may access your confidential information. It is also in your financial interest, because copying costs can be astronomical.

- **Fax costs**: As with the phone and copier, the fax can easily run up costs. Set a limit.

- **Postage charges**: Be aware of how much it costs to send a legal document overnight, or a registered letter. Offer to pick up or deliver expensive items when it makes sense.

- **Filing fees**: Make it clear to your attorney that you want to minimize the number of court filings in your case. Watch your bill and question any filing that seems unnecessary.

- **Document production fee**: Turning over documents to your opponent is mandatory and expensive. If you're faced with reproducing boxes of documents, consider having the job done by a commercial firm rather than your attorney's office.

- **Research and investigations**: Pay only for photographs that can be used in court. Can you hire a photographer at a lower rate than what your attorney charges? Reserve that right in your retainer agreement. Database research can also be extensive and expensive; if your attorney uses Westlaw or Nexis, set limits on the research you will pay for.

- **Expert witnesses**: Question your attorney if you are expected to pay for more than a reasonable number of expert witnesses. Limit the number to what is essential to your case.

- **Technology costs**: Avoid videos, tape recordings, and graphics if you can use old-fashioned diagrams to illustrate your case.

- **Travel expenses**: Travel expenses for those connected to your case can be quite costly unless you set a maximum budget. Check all travel-related items on your bill, and make sure they are appropriate. Always question why the travel is necessary before you agree to pay for it.

- **Appeals costs**: Losing a case often means an appeal, but weigh the costs involved before you make that decision. If money is at stake, do a cost-benefit analysis to see if an appeal is financially justified.

- **Monetary damages**: Your attorney should be able to help you estimate the total damages you will have to pay if you lose a civil case. Always consider settling out of court rather than proceeding to trial when the trial costs will be high.

- **Surprise costs**: Surprise costs are so routine they're predictable. The judge may impose unexpected court orders on one or both sides, or the opposition will file an unexpected motion that increases your legal costs. Budget a few thousand dollars over what you estimate your case will cost. It usually is needed.

- **Padded expenses**: Assume your costs and expenses are legitimate. But some firms do inflate expenses—office supplies, database searches, copying, postage, phone bills—to bolster their bottom line. Request copies of bills your law firm receives from support services. If you are not the only client represented on a bill, determine those charges related to your case.

Keeping it legal without a lawyer

The best way to save legal costs is to avoid legal problems. There are hundreds of ways to decrease your chances of lawsuits and other nasty legal encounters. Most simply involve a little common sense. You can also use your own initiative to find and use the variety of self-help legal aid available to consumers.

11 situations in which you may not need a lawyer

1) **No-fault divorce**: Married couples with no children, minimal property, and no demands for alimony can take advantage of divorce mediation services. A lawyer should review your divorce agreement before you sign it, but you will have saved a fortune in attorney fees. A marital or family counselor may save a seemingly doomed marriage, or help both parties move beyond anger to a calm settlement. Either way, counseling can save you money.

2) **Wills**: Do-it-yourself wills and living trusts are ideal for people with estates of less than $600,000. Even if an attorney reviews your final documents, a will kit allows you to read the documents, ponder your bequests, fill out sample forms, and discuss your wishes with your family at your leisure, without a lawyer's meter running.

3) **Incorporating**: Incorporating a small business can be done by any business owner. Your state government office provides the forms and instructions necessary. A visit to your state office will probably be

necessary to perform a business name check. A fee of $100-$200 is usually charged for processing your Articles of Incorporation. The rest is paperwork: filling out forms correctly; holding regular, official meetings; and maintaining accurate records.

4) **Routine business transactions**: Copyrights, for example, can be applied for by asking the U.S. Copyright Office for the appropriate forms and brochures. The same is true of the U.S. Patent and Trademark Office. If your business does a great deal of document preparation and research, hire a certified paralegal rather than paying an attorney's rates. Consider mediation or binding arbitration rather than going to court for a business dispute. Hire a human resources/benefits administrator to head off disputes concerning discrimination or other employee charges.

5) **Repairing bad credit**: When money matters get out of hand, attorneys and bankruptcy should not be your first solution. Contact a credit counseling organization that will help you work out manageable payment plans so that everyone wins. It can also help you learn to manage your money better. A good company to start with is the Consumer Credit Counseling Service, 1-800-388-2227.

6) **Small Claims Court**: For legal grievances amounting to a few thousand dollars in damages, represent yourself in Small Claims Court. There is a small filing fee, forms to fill out, and several court visits necessary. If you can collect evidence, state your case in a clear and logical presentation, and come across as neat, respectful and sincere, you can succeed in Small Claims Court.

7) **Traffic Court**: Like Small Claims Court, Traffic Court may show more compassion to a defendant appearing without an attorney. If you are ticketed for a minor offense and want to take it to court, you will be asked to plead guilty or not guilty. If you plead guilty, you can ask for leniency in sentencing by presenting mitigating circumstances. Bring any witnesses who can support your story, and remember that presentation (some would call it acting ability) is as important as fact.

8) **Residential zoning petition**: If a homeowner wants to open a home business, build an addition, or make other changes that may affect his or her neighborhood, town approval is required. But you don't need a lawyer to fill out a zoning variance application, turn it in, and present your story at a public hearing. Getting local support before the hearing is the best way to assure a positive vote; contact as many neighbors as possible to reassure them that your plans won't adversely affect them or the neighborhood.

9) **Government benefit applications**: Applying for veterans' or unemployment benefits may be daunting, but the process doesn't require legal help. Apply for either immediately upon becoming eligible. Note: If your former employer contests your application for unemployment benefits and you have to defend yourself at a hearing, you may want to consider hiring an attorney.

10) **Receiving government files**: The Freedom of Information Act gives every American the right to receive copies of government information about him or her. Write a letter to the appropriate state or federal agency, noting the precise information you want. List each document in a separate paragraph. Mention the Freedom of Information Act, and state that you will pay any expenses. Close with your signature and the address the documents should be sent to. An approved request may take six months to arrive. If it is refused on the grounds that the information is classified or violates another's privacy, send a letter of appeal explaining why the released information would not endanger anyone. Enlist the support of your local state or federal representative, if possible, to smooth the approval process.

11) **Citizenship**: Arriving in the United States to work and become a citizen is a process tangled in bureaucratic red tape, but it requires more perseverance than legal assistance. Immigrants can learn how to obtain a "Green Card," under what circumstances they can work, and what the requirements of citizenship are by contacting the Immigration Services or reading a good self-help book.

Save more; it's E-Z

When it comes to saving attorneys' fees, Made E-Z Products is the consumer's best friend. America's largest publisher of self-help legal products offers legally valid forms for virtually every situation. E-Z Legal Kits and the Made E-Z Guides which cover legal topics include all necessary forms and a simple-to-follow manual of instructions or a layman's book. Made E-Z Books are a library of forms and documents for everyday business and personal needs. Made E-Z Software provides those same forms on disk and CD for customized documents at the touch of the keyboard.

You can add to your legal savvy and your ability to protect yourself, your loved ones, your business and your property with a range of self-help legal titles available through Made E-Z Products.

Save On Legal Fees

Stock No.: BK311
$29.95 8.5" x 11"
500 pages Soft cover
ISBN 1-56382-311-X

Everyday Law Made E-Z

The book that saves legal fees every time it's opened.

Here, in *Everyday Law Made E-Z*, are fast answers to 90% of the legal questions anyone is ever likely to ask, such as:

- How can I control my neighbor's pet?
- Can I change my name?
- What is a common law marriage?
- When should I incorporate my business?
- Is a child responsible for his bills?
- Who owns a husband's gifts to his wife?
- How do I become a naturalized citizen?
- Should I get my divorce in Nevada?
- Can I write my own will?
- Who is responsible when my son drives my car?
- How can my uncle get a Green Card?
- What are the rights of a non-smoker?
- Do I have to let the police search my car?
- What is sexual harassment?
- When is euthanasia legal?
- What repairs must my landlord make?
- What's the difference between fair criticism and slander?
- When can I get my deposit back?
- Can I sue the federal government?
- Am I responsible for a drunken guest's auto accident?
- Is a hotel liable if it does not honor a reservation?
- Does my car fit the lemon law?

Whether for personal or business use, this 500-page information-packed book helps the layman safeguard his property, avoid disputes, comply with legal obligations, and enforce his rights. Hundreds of cases illustrate thousands of points of law, each clearly and completely explained.

MADE E-Z
PRODUCTS

Whatever you need to know, we've made it E-Z!

Informative text and forms you can fill out on-screen.* From personal to business, legal to leisure—we've made it E-Z!

PERSONAL & FAMILY

For all your family's needs, we have titles that will help keep you organized and guide you through most every aspect of your personal life.

BUSINESS

Whether you're starting from scratch with a home business or you just want to keep your corporate records in shape, we've got the programs for you.

FEDERAL & STATE
Labor Law Posters

The Poster 15 Million Businesses Must Have This Year!

All businesses must display federal labor laws at each location, or risk fines and penalties of up to $7,000!
And changes in September and October of 1997 made all previous Federal Labor Law Posters obsolete;
so make sure you're in compliance—use ours!

State	Item#	State	Item#	State	Item#
Alabama	83801	Louisiana	83818	Ohio	83835
Alaska	83802	Maine	83819	Oklahoma	83836
Arizona	83803	Maryland	83820	Oregon	83837
Arkansas	83804	Massachusetts	83821	Pennsylvania	83838
California	83805	Michigan	83822	Rhode Island	83839
Colorado	83806	Minnesota	83823	South Carolina	83840
Connecticut	83807	Mississippi	83824	South Dakota not available	
Delaware	83808	Missouri	83825	Tennessee	83842
Florida	83809	Montana	83826	Texas	83843
Georgia	83810	Nebraska	83827	Utah	83844
Hawaii	83811	Nevada	83828	Vermont	83845
Idaho	83812	New Hampshire	83829	Virginia	83846
Illinois	83813	New Jersey	83830	Washington	83847
Indiana	83814	New Mexico	83831	Washington, D.C.	83848
Iowa	83815	New York	83832	West Virginia	83849
Kansas	83816	North Carolina	83833	Wisconsin	83850
Kentucky	83817	North Dakota	83834	Wyoming	83851

State Labor Law Compliance Poster
Avoid up to $10,000 in fines by posting the
required State Labor Law Poster available from
Made E-Z Products.

$29.95

Federal Labor Law Poster
This colorful, durable 17³/₄" x 24" poster is in
full federal compliance and includes:

- The NEW Fair Labor Standards Act Effective
  October 1, 1996
  (New Minimum Wage Act)

- The Family & Medical Leave Act of 1993*

- The Occupational Safety and Health
  Protection Act of 1970

- The Equal Opportunity Act

- The Employee Polygraph Protection Act

* Businesses with fewer than 50 employees should display reverse
side of poster, which excludes this act.

$11.99
Stock No. LP001

See the order form in this guide to order yours today!

By the book...

MADE E·Z® LIBRARY

MADE E-Z GUIDES

Each comprehensive guide contains all the information you need to learn about one of dozens of topics, plus sample forms (if applicable).

Most guides also include an appendix of valuable resources, a handy glossary, and the valuable 14-page supplement "How to Save on Attorney Fees."

TITLES

Asset Protection Made E-Z
Shelter your property from financial disaster.

Bankruptcy Made E-Z
Take the confusion out of filing bankruptcy.

Buying/Selling a Business Made E-Z
Position your business and structure the deal for quick results.

Buying/Selling Your Home Made E-Z
Buy or sell your home for the right price right now!

Collecting Child Support Made E-Z
Ensure your kids the support they deserve.

Collecting Unpaid Bills Made E-Z
Get paid–and faster–every time.

Corporate Record Keeping Made E-Z
Minutes, resolutions, notices, and waivers for any corporation.

Credit Repair Made E-Z
All the tools to put you back on track.

Divorce Law Made E-Z
Learn to proceed on your own, without a lawyer.

Employment Law Made E-Z
A handy reference for employers and employees.

Everyday Law Made E-Z
Fast answers to 90% of your legal questions.

Everyday Legal Forms & Agreements Made E-Z
Personal and business protection for virtually any situation.

Incorporation Made E-Z
Information you need to get your company INC'ed.

Last Wills Made E-Z
Write a will the right way, the E-Z way.

Limited Liability Companies Made E-Z
Learn all about the hottest new business entity.

Living Trusts Made E-Z
Trust us to help you provide for your loved ones.

Living Wills Made E-Z
Take steps now to ensure Death with Dignity.

Managing Employees Made E-Z
Your own personnel director in a book.

Partnerships Made E-Z
Get your company started the right way.

Small Claims Court Made E-Z
Prepare for court...or explore other avenues.

Traffic Court Made E-Z
Learn your rights on the road and in court.

Solving IRS Problems Made E-Z
Settle with the IRS for pennies on the dollar.

Trademarks & Copyrights Made E-Z
How to obtain your own copyright or trademark.

Vital Record Keeping Made E-Z
Preserve vital records and important information.

KITS

Each kit includes a clear, concise instruction manual to help you understand your rights and obligations, plus all the information and sample forms you need.

For the busy do-it-yourselfer, it's quick, affordable, and it's E-Z.

	Item#	Qty.	Price Ea.‡
E✦Z Legal Kits			
Bankruptcy	K100		$23.95
Incorporation	K101		$23.95
Divorce	K102		$29.95
Credit Repair	K103		$21.95
Living Trust	K105		$21.95
Living Will	K106		$23.95
Last Will & Testament	K107		$18.95
Buying/Selling Your Home	K111		$21.95
Employment Law	K112		$21.95
Collecting Child Support	K115		$21.95
Limited Liability Company	K116		$21.95
Made E✦Z Software			
Accounting Made E-Z	SW1207		$29.95
Asset Protection Made E-Z	SW1157		$29.95
Bankruptcy Made E-Z	SW1154		$29.95
Best Career Oppportunities Made E-Z	SW1216		$29.95
Brain-Buster Crossword Puzzles	SW1223		$29.95
Brain-Buster Jigsaw Puzzles	SW1222		$29.95
Business Startups Made E-Z	SW1192		$29.95
Buying/Selling Your Home Made E-Z	SW1213		$29.95
Car Buying Made E-Z	SW1146		$29.95
Corporate Record Keeping Made E-Z	SW1159		$29.95
Credit Repair Made E-Z	SW1153		$29.95
Divorce Law Made E-Z	SW1182		$29.95
Everyday Law Made E-Z	SW1185		$29.95
Everyday Legal Forms & Agreements	SW1186		$29.95
Incorporation Made E-Z	SW1176		$29.95
Last Wills Made E-Z	SW1177		$29.95
Living Trusts Made E-Z	SW1178		$29.95
Offshore Investing Made E-Z	SW1218		$29.95
Owning a Franchise Made E-Z	SW1202		$29.95
Touring Florence, Italy Made E-Z	SW1220		$29.95
Touring London, England Made E-Z	SW1221		$29.95
Vital Record Keeping Made E-Z	SW1160		$29.95
Website Marketing Made E-Z	SW1203		$29.95
Your Profitable Home Business	SW1204		$29.95
Made E✦Z Guides			
Bankruptcy Made E-Z	G200		$17.95
Incorporation Made E-Z	G201		$17.95
Divorce Law Made E-Z	G202		$17.95
Credit Repair Made E-Z	G203		$17.95
Living Trusts Made E-Z	G205		$17.95
Living Wills Made E-Z	G206		$17.95
Last Wills Made E-Z	G207		$17.95
Small Claims Court Made E-Z	G209		$17.95
Traffic Court Made E-Z	G210		$17.95
Buying/Selling Your Home Made E-Z	G211		$17.95
Employment Law Made E-Z	G212		$17.95
Collecting Child Support Made E-Z	G215		$17.95
Limited Liability Companies Made E-Z	G216		$17.95
Partnerships Made E-Z	G218		$17.95
Solving IRS Problems Made E-Z	G219		$17.95
Asset Protection Secrets Made E-Z	G220		$17.95
Immigration Made E-Z	G223		$17.95
Buying/Selling a Business Made E-Z	G223		$17.95
Made E✦Z Books			
Managing Employees Made E-Z	BK308		$29.95
Corporate Record Keeping Made E-Z	BK310		$29.95
Vital Record Keeping Made E-Z	BK312		$29.95
Business Forms Made E-Z	BK313		$29.95
Collecting Unpaid Bills Made E-Z	BK309		$29.95
Everyday Law Made E-Z	BK311		$29.95
Everyday Legal Forms & Agreements	BK307		$29.95
Labor Posters			
Federal Labor Law Poster	LP001		$11.99
State Labor Law Poster (specify state)			$29.95
Shipping & Handling*			$
TOTAL OF ORDER:**			$

See an item in this book you would like to order?

To order :
1. Photocopy this order form.
2. Use the photocopy to complete your order and mail to:

MADE E-Z PRODUCTS

384 S Military Trail, Deerfield Beach, FL 33442
phone: (954) 480-8933 ✦ fax: (954) 480-8906
web site: http://www.e-zlegal.com/

‡Prices current as of 10/99

Shipping and Handling: Add $3.50 for the first item, $1.50 for each additional item.

**Florida residents add 6% sales tax.

Total payment must accompany all orders.
Make checks payable to: Made E-Z Products, Inc.

NAME _____

COMPANY _____

ORGANIZATION _____

_____

ADDRESS _____

CITY _____ STATE _____ ZIP _____

PHONE ( ) _____

PAYMENT:

❏ CHECK ENCLOSED, PAYABLE TO MADE E-Z PRODUCTS, INC.

❏ PLEASE CHARGE MY ACCOUNT: ❏ MasterCard ❏ VISA

EXP DATE

ACCOUNT NO.

Signature: _____
(required for credit card purchases)

-OR-

For faster service, order by phone:
(954) 480-8933

Or you can fax your order to us:
(954) 480-8906

SS 1999 r2

Index

M-P♦♦♦♦♦

Q-W♦♦♦♦♦